THE COMPLETE GUIDE TO
EDITORIAL FREELANCING

*the text of this book is printed
on 100% recycled paper*

THE COMPLETE GUIDE TO EDITORIAL FREELANCING

Carol L. O'Neill
Avima Ruder

◇◇

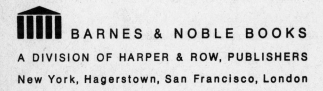 BARNES & NOBLE BOOKS

A DIVISION OF HARPER & ROW, PUBLISHERS

New York, Hagerstown, San Francisco, London

A hardcover edition of this book is published by Dodd, Mead & Company.
It is here reprinted by arrangement.

First BARNES & NOBLE BOOKS edition published 1979

ISBN: 0-06-463473-6

79 80 81 82 83 10 9 8 7 6 5 4 3 2 1

To all freelancers, in the hope that they will someday get the recognition — and pay — they deserve

ACKNOWLEDGMENTS

The following copy editors, editors, and writers were kind enough to review our manuscript in its preparatory stages: Zahava Feldman; Denny Fowler; Walter Fox; Laura Horowitz and Editorial Experts; Richard Lehman; Barbara Palumbo; Janice Pargh; Claire Sanford Perrault; Beth Salter; Robert Woodward; Gretchen Zollendeck. Thanks also to Miriam Ruder, Barbara Siemann, and Maureen Laino for "volunteering" to help proofread and to send out questionnaires; to Doris Berger and Bettylou Rosen for the librarian's point of view. And to Peter Weed and Sabra Doumlele of Dodd, Mead, and to innumerable relatives, friends, and acquaintances, our thanks for goading us into not only starting but also finishing this book.

Special thanks to Milton Waldman and Lewis Manheimer of the Internal Revenue Service, who patiently reviewed the chapter on taxes.

And to all the freelancers who took the time to answer our questionnaires—may they all prosper: Joseph Alverez; Margaret Neal Anderson; Martha Anderson; Charles E. Andrews; N. J. Anthony; Sylvia Antonier-Scher; Alice and Haig Assatourian; Astor Indexers; Sylvia Auerbach; Author Aid Associates; Author's Guidance Service; Janet H. Baker; Bernice Balfour; Riva Bandler; Diana Barth; David J. Baruch; Dorothy Beck; Anita Beckerman; Saretta Berlin; Helen Freud Bernays; Joseph M. Bernstein; Philip Biddison; Marjorie M. Bitker; Gilbert J. Black; Ruth R. Borden; Eileen Brand; Elsa Branden; Norman Howard Brown; Alan Caruba; Curtis W. Casewit; Charles Irwin Choset; Mrs. Glenn Clairmonte; Frances G. Conn; Norma Crandall; Creative Services; Robert M. Cullers; Louella S.

Culligan; Robert Daugherty; Charles Decker; Mary A. DeVries; Corinne Dickey; Betty J. T. Drenkhahn; Editorial Consultants; Editorial Services; Henry W. Engel; Nan C. Fahy; Judith Falco; Ann Finlayson; Mary M. Flad; Theodore P. Francis; Peggy Lois French; Martha M. Garlin; Irene Glynn; Hadassah Gold; Ellen Gordon; Leona W. Greenhill; Betty Herr Hallinger; Raymond Hamilton; James E. Hartman; Harriett; Herr's Indexing Service; Laurice House; Eva M. Hunte; Curt Johnson; Dr. Jerome H. Kanner; Dana Frank Kellerman; Roy Craik Kollenborn; Mary Krull; Ellie Kurtz; Robert Levin; Leon H. Lewis; Peter Limburg; Ruth Norden Lowe; Nancy MacKenzie; Walter MacPeek; Libby Machol; Bruce Macomber; Gilbert R. Magee; Tom Mahoney; Judith Mansfield; H. K. Marer Associates; Genevieve B. Mason; Lisa McGaw; Helen McGrath; Anne V. McGravie; Kathleen McLaughlin; Nancy McNulty; Morton J. Merowitz; Robert J. Milch; Sondra Roth Mochson; Francis B. Morrison Editorial Service; Marye Myers; Bill Newgold; Edith H. Nolder; Anne Norton; Ann Novotny; Elsa G. Nugent; Phyllis Old; Elizabeth O'Neil; Robert J. Palmer; Esther I. Persson; Agnes D. Peters; Professional Editing and Typing Services; Ray Editorial Services; Research Reports; Peter Rooney; Betty J. Russell; Harold J. Salemson; Dorothy Sara; Mira Schachne; Anita A. Schenck; Science Bookcrafters, Inc.; Science Consultants; Hope M. Scrogin; Doris P. Shalley; Margot Shields; Lucille Simpson; Saul D. Slaff; Diane Sloves; Carolyn Smith; Julia Stair; Eleanor F. Steiner-Prag; Katherine Stelsky; Martha Jane Sternberg; Alfred Stevens; Joseph Tell; P. K. Thomajan; Phyllis Tuma; Frances Von Maltitz; Del Walker; Florence E. Wall; Henrietta Weigel; Rose Weinberg; Virginia Wharton; Rachel Whitebook; Robert H. Wilcox; Lynda Wildman; Helen Stroop Witty; Writers: Free-Lance, Inc.

Carol L. O' Neill and Avima Ruder

FOREWORD TO THE PAPERBACK EDITION

The grass has never been greener for editorial freelancers. Since the publication of the first edition of this *Guide,* publishers have responded to broad economic conditions by minimizing the number of in-house employees and by expanding the role and image of paperback books in the industry. The combined effect of these two trends has been to enlarge significantly the freelance job market.

Over the past several years freelance copyediting and proofreading jobs have proliferated as in-house departments have shrunk. And while those two skills, along with indexing, still comprise the bulk of freelanced editorial work, the versatile freelancer can now choose from a wider variety of jobs. Publishers are freelancing production editing as never before, and paperback houses in particular are farming out unprecedented amounts of manuscript reading, editing, and rewriting. With these more lucrative assignments flowing into the freelance market, the editorial freelancer need no longer trade wages for freedom.

THE EDITORS

CONTENTS

THE COMPLETE GUIDE TO
EDITORIAL FREELANCING

Chapter 1

AVOIDING THE RUSH HOUR

IN OLDEN days the "free lance" sold his military skills to the highest bidder. The legacy of these industrious mercenaries continues today in the legion of editorial freelancers who offer their literary talents to publishers, thus of course proving that the pen is mightier than the sword.

Editorial freelancing is a serious, moneymaking business. But more than that, it is great fun and full of excitement, and it provides an opportunity to take an active yet independent role in the publishing industry. A freelancer should love books; should chortle with glee if she [1] finds and corrects a misplaced comma or creates a useful, well-organized index; should yearn to make every manuscript a great book. Although freelancing is a job, it can—and should—be a creative, self-satisfying experience.

With this in mind, *The Complete Guide to Editorial Freelancing* covers all aspects of freelancing—the various specialties, the specific work each specialist does, the ways to get first and repeat assignments,

[1] At the risk of irritating male chauvinists, we have identified freelancers, editors, and authors as "she,"'since the majority are female and the pronoun is handy.

1

setting up an office, keeping records for tax returns—in as light a vein as possible. This book is meant to be read and enjoyed; it was not conceived as a manual where the index will be the most thumb-worn pages. There are invaluable reference works—dictionaries and style manuals in particular—which a freelancer must own. But *The Complete Guide to Editorial Freelancing* is intended to serve as a pleasurable learning experience for new freelancers and for current freelancers who wish to learn another freelancing specialty. In addition, this book provides a memory-jogging review of intricacies for current freelancers; and the sample copyediting and proofreading tests in Appendix IV offer practice and feedback for both novice and experienced freelancers. Who among us remembers everything?

No one knows the number of full- and part-time freelancers, for they work independently, usually for more than one publisher. Their editorial skills range from copyediting, proofreading, and indexing—the big three—to manuscript reading and evaluating, research, translating, picture research and editing, manuscript typing, and writing captions and jacket copy. An individual may specialize in one of these fields or may be competent in many areas. (Besides editorial freelancers, there are freelance writers, editors, and designers, whose work is not specifically discussed in this book.)

Publishers use editorial freelancers primarily because of the large pool of talent available. A textbook on electrical engineering, for example, should be copyedited by someone with knowledge in that field. Who else could spot possible errors? A songbook must be proofread by someone who can read music. A cookbook indexer should know that "tomato" must not be listed under "vegetable." Publishers maintain lists of freelancers and call on the particular person they believe best suited for the manuscript at hand.

Large publishing houses are commonly split into divisions handling particular kinds of books. The most usual divisions are trade books (general adult and children's fiction and nonfiction), reference books, and textbooks (which may be divided further into college, high school, and elementary; or "el-hi" may be combined). Each division usually has its own list of freelancers.

Many publishers have staff personnel who copy-edit, proofread, index, or handle the other jobs a free-lancer can do. But the publishing industry has peak seasons when many books are in the works, followed by sluggish periods. It is uneconomical to hire the number of full-time employees needed in the rush season and then pay them to sit around and look busy when the work slacks off.

Most books come on the market either in the spring or in the fall. Generally it takes at least six months for a manuscript to be transformed into a book, so peak seasons for editorial work are in the fall (for spring books) and in the spring (for fall books). July, August, January, and February are usually months of diminished work for freelancers.

The basic procedure for the transformation of a manuscript into a book is as follows:

1) Manuscript is accepted by publisher, perhaps after critical evaluation by expert.

2) Translator may be needed.
3) Manuscript is assigned to an editor, who edits it (which may involve extensive rewriting or reorganizing).
4) Researcher may be asked to check all facts and figures.
5) Book jacket is designed, jacket copy is written.
6) Manuscript may be retyped.
7) Manuscript is copyedited.
8) Manuscript is sent to compositor (typesetter) to be set in type.
9) Galleys are received from compositor and are proofread.
10) Galleys are returned to compositor; indicated changes are made and the type is then divided into pages.
11) Page proofs are received from compositor and editorial changes are proofread.
12) Index is prepared.
13) Index is sent to compositor to be set in type, is returned, and is proofread.
14) Book is mechanically put together and copies are sent to publisher.
15) Book is distributed and becomes instant best seller.

Because each step from typesetting to packaging the books for distribution may take place in a different plant, or in a different section of the same plant, and because proofs and samples must be sent to the publisher's production and editorial departments at each stage, producing a book takes a great deal of time—six months is usually the *minimum*.

PROS AND CONS OF FREELANCING

A freelancer is a self-employed individual, freed from the monotony of the nine-to-five office routine, freed from office politics, freed from having to waste hours in hectic commuting. She can set her own pace and establish her own time schedule. The night person can get up at noon and freelance into the wee hours. The day person can start at dawn and quit in time to visit a museum and have an early dinner. A freelancer can work sixteen straight hours on a fascinating book if she so chooses; she can work two hours at a stretch if the book is dull. The deadline for the book must be met, but when the work is done is entirely up to the freelancer. Part-time freelancers can fit work around children and home or another full-time job.

A freelancer can specialize in one editorial area, such as copyediting or indexing. She can specialize in one subject of particular interest, making herself available to enough publishers to get an adequate supply of work. The more areas of expertise the freelancer has, the better her chances of having a good supply of assignments.

Freelancing is not a career conducive to living in luxury, but there is money to be made, especially if the freelancer can supplement proofreading and copyediting with more lucrative editing and writing jobs. As a freelancer gains experience, she can make the personal contacts necessary to upgrade her earnings. For tax purposes, part of the rent or mortgage payments, part of the phone bill, transportation and mailing charges, and similar expenses are subtracted from the gross (see Chapter 7). There is definitely work available for the person who is competent, thorough, and able to meet deadlines. Assignments will not continue, however, for the freelancer who is less than competent, slipshod, and insensitive to due dates.

The main difficulty encountered by freelancers is a "feast or famine" workload. During peak seasons the freelancer may have no choice but to refuse work, for she may be laboring twelve hours a day, five or six or even seven days a week. Then the work tapers off or ends abruptly and terrible thoughts occur: Have I done a bad job? Will the publisher ever call again? Where's the rent money coming from? Just as suddenly, the work is likely to pick up. Publishers usually do not contact a freelancer in advance; the day the book is ready to be sent out, they try to find someone to do it. Thus the freelancer cannot schedule her time for more than a few weeks in advance. And she knows that if she turns down a publisher too often, her name is likely to be stricken from its all-important list. This inherent uncertainty can trap a freelancer in a vicious circle: She may take too much work, for fear of not having enough. She is then likely to do an unsatisfactory job and not get any more calls from that particular publisher. It is far preferable to recommend a competent freelancer friend than to accept more than you can handle.

The authors of this book firmly believe that publishers should try to arrange assignments in advance. Also, we believe that some personal contact between freelancers and publishing house personnel would be beneficial—perhaps an hour meeting once or twice a year, or even a lunch. An editor at UCLA Press suggests inviting freelancers to a Christmas party.[2] The freelancer then becomes a flesh-and-blood person, not a telephone voice and a name on a bill; the editors become people with a hectic schedule, working on many books and not always able to take time to congratulate a freelancer for a job well done, or even to remember who did which book. When possible, a freelancer should personally pick up and/or deliver a book, so that she will have *some* personal contact.

Lack of communication is another major peeve of freelancers. Publishers frequently do not give detailed instructions, even when they are deviating from standard editorial procedures. Or they may set early deadlines to ensure the timely return of a manuscript, forcing the conscientious freelancer to slave away to meet the deadline. Then the delivered manuscript sits around the publishing house for a week or so, unopened.

Freelancers on occasion complain of loneliness, of being cut off from the mainstream of publishing—and from human contact. There is no organization where freelancers can meet to talk shop and exchange experiences, to share triumphs and gripes. (Indexers are fortunate, however, for the Society of Indexers, which started in England, has formed a group in the United States.) It is rare that a freelancer gets direct comment on her completed work. Repeat assignments are the thank you for a job satisfactorily or magnificently done. Thus the freelancer must be able

[2] James E. Kubeck, "The Freelance System Works for Us," *Scholarly Publishing*, April 1972, pp. 268–72.

to judge her own work more than an in-house employee, and provide her own criticism when she has done less than her best and her own praise when she knows she deserves it.

Money matters are another peeve. There are no raises based on experience and expertise. A novice freelancer generally cannot work as quickly or as accurately as a seasoned pro. Yet both normally receive the same hourly rate, a standard amount paid by the publisher. The experienced freelancer is in effect being penalized for her speed. This has led almost all freelancers to pad their bills based on an average amount of work per hour (see Chapter 2). Slowness of payment is another frequent complaint of freelancers. Generally a check can be expected in two or three weeks. Occasionally it takes a month or even two. Some publishers do not seem to understand that unlike their printers or paper suppliers, freelancers are individuals who may be waiting for a check to pay the rent or to buy groceries.

Finally, freelancers frequently complain of neighbors, friends, and relatives intruding on their work time. It is necessary for a freelancer to impress on others that although she is at home, she is *working*— not vacuuming for the umpteenth time or engrossed in TV or engaged in some other activity she would gladly drop. Just as an in-house employee cannot chat endlessly on the phone, so the freelancer is not able to receive callers at all hours.

Publishers' peeves about freelancers are quite basic: sloppy, inaccurate work and missed deadlines. One publisher summed up the situation succinctly: A good freelancer is hard to find.

Chapter 2

A FOOT IN THE DOOR

Having read about the pros—and cons—
of freelancing, and yet continuing to read, you must
still be interested in becoming part of this mad
world. Most people are at least roughly acquainted
with the mechanics of finding an office job (writing
directly to the firm one would like to work for, or
visiting an employment agency), but even those who
have worked in publishing for years often have no
idea how to gain freelance assignments. Before you
plunge in as a freelancer, take a tentative dip. If you
are now a full-time permanent employee, either in
publishing or in another field, *do not quit and then
start looking for freelance editorial work.* Even freelancers with years of experience have fallow periods;
a beginner may have an even rougher time. Start
small: Write to several firms, do some freelancing in
the evening or on weekends. Many freelancers start
out this way, intending to quit their permanent jobs,
but never get around to it! Some discover that they
do not have the discipline or temperament to be freelancers; some continue moonlighting as freelancers.
Most likely you do not want to work sixty hours a
week forever. But it will not kill you to do it for a

while. You will gain experience, confidence, and, perhaps most important, *contacts*.

PERSONAL CONTACTS

Those magic words: personal contacts. Once you have established a reputation as a reliable, competent freelancer at a few publishing houses, you can count on a fairly constant flow of work. You will be even better off if you get to know personally, and be respected by, a few copy chiefs and production editors. If your liaison moves to another job, you will still have contacts with her old firm, plus an acquaintance now at yet another publishing house. Publishing personnel are peripatetic, so within a few years you may build up a network of job sources.

How do you get to know these editors in the first place? About one sixth of the freelancers who answered the questionnaire sent out for this book stated that they had been introduced by friends to "handers-out" of freelance work; over half of the respondents had worked in publishing houses before they started freelancing. Naturally it helps if someone introduces you to a copy chief, although after your first assignment you must expect to be judged on your merits rather than as "Gwendolyn's friend Cecily."

A friend can also help by allowing you to have a first crack at one of her own assignments. Then, after doing the job herself, she can go over the work with you. Your report of her careful tutoring will make her a doubly good reference for you, and she may even be willing to turn over part of her fee to you, although since the bill would be in her name and she therefore would have to pay tax on the amount, unless she listed you in her tax records as the "subcontractor," do not expect her to keep doing such favors. Anyway, once you have some "real" experience you should be able to go ahead on your own merits.

If you know no one in publishing, check "Editorial Work—Free Lance" in *Literary Market Place*, the "phone book" of publishing, for freelancers in your region. Try writing to ask their advice. The same section of *LMP* lists freelancing organizations, started by groups of freelancers who banded together, or by one person who constantly was asked to do more work than she could handle, and so began to farm out work to other freelancers. These organizations may be looking for more freelancers to help handle their workloads; get in touch with them. *Literary Market Place* is issued in yearly editions by R. R. Bowker, and can be ordered by mail (Bowker, PO Box 1807, Ann Arbor, Michigan 48106).

CASTING ARROWS

If you do not know anyone who "knows anyone," head for the typewriter. Send a letter and resume to every publishing house in your area that may use freelancers. Better to send too many letters than too few, for a large percentage of your "arrows" will surely miss the mark. Publishers are listed in your local Yellow Pages. All United States publishers are also listed in *LMP*, and foreign publishers in *International LMP*.

If your inquiries about freelance work are not answered or result in a "we never use freelancers" reply, try again in a few months.

A firm using staff in 1979 may decide to hire freelancers to do the job in 1980. One source of such useful tidbits of professional gossip is *Publishers Weekly,* the trade journal of publishing. Another job source is *Freelancer's Newsletter.* This semimonthly six-to eight-page bulletin lists some editorial freelance jobs, although most are for writers or artists. One useful feature is "The Going Rate." Readers anonymously report fees paid for various editorial chores. See Appendix II for complete information on both periodicals.

Other sources for editorial freelance work, in addition to book publishers, include: magazine and newspaper publishers; advertising agencies; associations that produce newsletters, annual reports, or brochures; governmental agencies that issue bulletins or consumer reports; local organizations, such as church groups (although they may want "amateurs" rather than paid professionals). If you have some expertise in a field, write to appropriate local, state, and national professional societies. An expert on American history, for example, may find that the committee for a local historic landmark needs someone to revise and pep up the prose in its information leaflet; or a busy history professor at a local college may have a book manuscript awaiting editing or indexing. Be imaginative in exploring all those areas that may yield freelance assignments.

Every possible aspect of editorial work is handled by freelancers, from typing to translating, research to rewrite. The big three—copyediting, proofreading, and indexing—and the others are discussed in detail in the following four chapters. If your lifelong interest in literature or journalism has given you the notion that you want to work in publishing, but you are not sure what area you like best or what you are best qualified for—or are at all qualified for—read about the various jobs and decide which will fit your personality and talents. Indexing and research are probably for the most meticulous minds; if you like doing puzzles, either of these may be your forte. Proofreading requires the ability to follow predetermined style and not impose your own ideas on the manuscript. Copyediting is much more creative than proofreading, although it is not equivalent to writing. Manuscript reading requires expertise in a particular field and excellent judgment. Translating is creative but painstaking. Jacket copy writing must be flamboyantly succinct—not an easy task. Typing is the most routine of all freelance jobs, but it offers an opportunity to do some copyediting tasks and is a fine way to get a key in the freelancing door, especially for those would-be freelancers without a college degree and/or publishing experience.

When approaching a publisher "cold" you should send a concise covering letter and a resume. *Proofread* both of these several times. If possible, have someone else look them over as well. Nothing will kill your chances faster than applying for an editorial job with a letter and resume containing errors in spelling or grammar.

THE HOLE TRUTH

There is quite a technique to organizing a resume so as to put your best foot forward. Consider the following application letters and resumes for three hypothetical freelancers with varying backgrounds: Susan Laurens, until recently a full-time editorial production assistant, can afford to be straightforward about her achievements. Miriam Samuels, who worked in publishing years ago but retired to raise a family, and Leonard Claire, who has a lot of work experience but none of it in publishing, must be more artful.

Being artful does not mean being untruthful—do not lie on a resume. If you are not a college graduate, do not say that you are; if you were fired for incompetence, do not say you quit. One of the authors of this book once worked in a magazine advertising department that needed a secretary. A particular applicant for the job stated she had been a Fulbright scholar. Resumes are rarely checked, but exaggerations are dangerous. At the cost of a phone call to California, the ad manager learned the applicant had merely been recommended for a Fulbright by one of her professors. This applicant got caught because of her apparent *overqualification* for the job. People in publishing switch jobs a lot. What if a former boss gets a copy of your overly creative resume?

Unpleasant facts should remain unmentioned, not be rewritten. For example, Miriam Samuels last worked in 1960. She simply avoids giving the date in her resume. In writing a resume you should always eliminate the negative and accentuate the positive—

2080 Madison Avenue
New York, N.Y. 10037
March 8, 1979

Chief Copy Editor
Michael Faraday & Company
777 Fifth Avenue
New York, N.Y. 10028

Dear Editor:

I am interested in doing copyediting and indexing on a freelance basis.
I have been freelancing full-time since last September and charge $5.50
an hour for both copyediting and indexing. A brief resume is enclosed.

Among the books I have worked on recently:

R. Van Rijn: LIGHT AND SHADOW, ART AND POLITICS IN THE NETHERLANDS,
    Chiaroscuro Press (indexed)

E. Bennett: SNOBS AND SUPERSNOBS, Austen House (copyedited)

H.D. Thoreau: LIVE ALONE AND LIKE IT, Concord and Lexington (copyedited
    and indexed)

P. Heidippides: I WALKED THE LAST MILE, Marathon Press (indexed)

I look forward to hearing from you.

                                    Sincerely,

                                    Susan Laurens

                                    Susan Laurens

Telephone: 123-4567

Susan Laurens
2080 Madison Avenue
New York, N.Y. 10037
123-4567

EXPERIENCE:

1972-present   Full-time freelance copy editor and indexer.

1969-72   Adult Trade Department, Austen House, New York City.
                    I copyedited jacket and catalog copy and most of the
                    nonfiction manuscripts. I also wrote some flap copy
                    and fact sheets. My duties included proofreading page
                    proofs, reproduction proofs, blueprints and color proofs;
                    checking jacket mechanicals and blueprints; preparing
                    detailed permissions records for all books; trafficking
                    all production details for new books and reprints.

                    I indexed many Austen House books on a freelance basis
                    and did additional freelance work for other publishers.

1967-69   Mudpie Magazine for Children, Philadelphia. I was re-
                    sponsible for copyediting and proofreading stories and
                    articles. I also handled reader inquiries addressed to
                    the magazine and set up and ran the "Junior Jingles"
                    column of poems sent in by young readers.

EDUCATION: B.A., Art History, 1967, University of Transylvania.

SPECIAL INTERESTS: Fine arts and architecture; camping; crafts and carpentry.

REFERENCES: M. E. Perkins
                    Editor-in-Chief
                    Austen House
                    1800 Regency Drive
                    New York, N.Y. 10048

                    Charles Dodgson
                    Managing Editor
                    Mudpie Magazine for Children
                    1789 Franklin Boulevard
                    Philadelphia, Pa. 19101

1066 Norman Road
Williams, Arizona 77766
July 5, 1979

Editor
University of Grand Canyon Press
PO Box 25
Flagstaff, Arizona 75432

Dear Editor:

I am interested in doing freelance copyediting, proofreading, and typing. Since leaving full-time publishing work I have done occasional freelance jobs, particularly typing and editing theses for doctoral candidates. Now that both my children attend school all day, I have more time available to freelance.

According to <u>Literary Market Place</u>, the University of Grand Canyon Press specializes in books about Southwestern history. American history, especially concerning this region of the country, has always been one of my chief interests. I would be delighted to work on such books.

Sincerely,

Miriam Samuels

Miriam Samuels

Telephone: (010) UC 1-2323

MIRIAM SAMUELS

EXPERIENCE: Associate Editor, Best Basic Books, Phoenix, Arizona.

I was responsible for all details of editorial work and
production on a series of texts for the primary and inter-
mediate grades. My duties included copyediting, layout,
scheduling, sending material to and from the printer, and
proofreading all stages from galleys to blueprints. In
addition, I edited a set of workbooks intended to comple-
ment the textbook series.

While working at BBB, and since leaving--when I married--
I have done some freelance copyediting, proofreading, and
typing.

EDUCATION: B.A., Education major, English minor, Gotham City College,
Flagstaff, 1956. Phi Beta Kappa.

As managing editor of the college newspaper, supervising a
staff of over fifty copy editors and proofreaders, I received
a tuition scholarship in lieu of salary.

SPECIAL INTERESTS: Education, American history and economics, home arts and
management.

REFERENCES: J. J. Dewey, Managing Editor
Best Basic Books
1950 Montessori Avenue
Phoenix, Arizona 76767

Professor Roger Bacon
Chairman, Metaphysics Department
University of the Southwest
Alamogordo, New Mexico 79997

1066 Norman Road
Williams, Arizona 77766

(010) UC 1-2323

6049 South Jersey
Chicago, Illinois 60645
December 9, 1979

Editor-in-Chief
<u>Illinois Isolationist</u>
PO Box 1812
Evanston, Illinois 60006

Dear Editor:

I am interested in doing typing and proofreading for your magazine, on a
freelance basis. A brief resume is enclosed.

I recently typed a manuscript soon to be published by Burning Bush Press:
FARMS AND FARM ANIMALS IN RESIDENTAL AREAS--A Study in Zoning Restrictions,
by Margaret O'Leary.

I hope to hear from you soon.

                                        Sincerely,

                                        Leonard Claire

                                        Leonard Claire

Telephones: IR 8-3038 (residence)
              910-1111 (office)

Leonard Claire

6049 South Jersey
IR 8-3038 (residence)
910-1111 (office)

EXPERIENCE:

1970-present   I am a freelance typist of court proceedings and
                    witnesses' depositions. Working from a court re-
                    porter's notes and tape recordings, I transcribe
                    the testimony and then proofread my typing. One
                    hundred percent accuracy is essential for these
                    legal proceedings.

1958-70   I typed and proofread transcripts of court pro-
                    ceedings and other legal processes as part of my
                    responsibilities as office manager for the official
                    court reporter for Federal Judge Ignatius Foot of
                    the Chicago District Court.

EDUCATION: I attended Northern University and the University
                    of Hyde Park as a part-time evening student majoring
                    in political science.

REFERENCES: O. W. Holmes IV
                    Federal District Judge
                    United States Courthouse
                    State and Van Buren Streets
                    Chicago, Illinois 60601

                    Marvin Boley, Attorney-at-Law
                    2001 Gold Coast Boulevard
                    Chicago, Illinois 60606

SPECIAL INTERESTS: Travel, classical music, political affairs, basketball,
                    and mountain climbing.

as Leonard Claire does on his resume by stressing experience relevant to publishing.

In your resume do not just list firms, job title, and term of employment. An "editorial assistant" may have duties ranging from those of a not-so-glorified secretary-typist to second-in-command of an entire department. Spell out your duties. If you assumed more and more responsibilities after some time on the job, say so. If your responsibilities were great but your title lowly, include your duties but not your title in the resume.

Former employers are always the best professional references, emphatically proving that you did not leave under a cloud. Ask permission from any person before giving him as a reference. It would be quite embarrassing, at the least, if someone got a call about you and said: "Beverly *who?*" If possible, get a typed letter of reference before you leave a job. Your immediate supervisor (the one you have listed as a reference) may leave, or the firm may be absorbed by a conglomerate, or may go out of business. One free-lancer got her start when the publishers she had been working for as a typist went bankrupt. The president passed out letters of reference praising *every* employee as a highly able senior editor.

Do not clutter your resume with irrelevant information, unless your professional background is so meager you must somehow piece out the resume. Do not write about your collegiate triumphs as student government president (but *do* mention your editorship of the school paper, until you have solid professional experience to replace it); do not mention your excellent health, or your two children (although they may be relevant if you are applying to edit child psychology texts).

Your concise, coherent covering letter should be slanted toward the firm you are approaching and addressed to the person who hands out the work you seek. A phone call to the firm will usually get you that person's name. If the company specializes in cookbooks and you are a master chef, mention it in your letter (see the Miriam Samuels letter for a sample of this approach). Use the covering letter to update your resume, including the books you have worked on most recently.

MADISON AVENUE APPROACH

Instead of sending out loads of letters and resumes, you might consider publicizing your availability. Or, having gotten started, you might advertise to keep your name before the eyes of publishing personnel. Some ad media are listed below. You might also advertise in a local college paper, especially if you are a typist, or in the classified ads section of a newspaper.

Literary Market Place listings of freelancers are *free*. To qualify for a listing send your name, address, and telephone number, plus three references from publishers you have worked for, to R. R. Bowker, 1180 Sixth Avenue, New York, N.Y. 10036. The final deadline for each year's edition is April (the new edition comes out at the end of June), but you can send in your listing application at any time. Bowker will keep it on file until January or February, when they start sending out questionnaires to freelancers.

Publishers Weekly ad rates may be obtained from the

publisher, at 1180 Sixth Avenue, New York, N.Y. 10036, and they are not prohibitive for most freelancers. The deadline for any week's edition is Wednesday noon twelve days before publication, or Tuesday for weeks with holidays. *PW* is also a Bowker publication.

Writer's Digest accepts ads from manuscript typists. Your order should include a sample page of typing as well as payment. The deadline is two months in advance for each month's issue. (*Writer's Digest*, 9933 Alliance Road, Cincinnati, Ohio 45242.)

GETTING STARTED

As in so many other fields, publishers generally require publishing experience before they will give you publishing experience. It would seem to be even harder for freelancers to break in, but an amazing one third of freelancers answering our questionnaires never held jobs in publishing! Many started by typing dissertations or indexing books for an author who did not want to do it himself. One freelancer began manuscript typing to help put her daughter through college. She discovered how faulty many manuscripts were, and she "could not seem to send them back to their authors without needed corrections. This grew into wider work with manuscripts." Another enterprising freelancer started out reading play scripts, was asked for editorial help by the playwrights submitting scripts, and soon got into freelance editing and rewriting.

Any kind of work that uses editorial skills, whether or not it has anything to do with publishing, might lead to editorial jobs. Teachers who correct student themes are editing; librarians who classify books are indexing. Anyone who has ever researched and written a term paper has exercised editorial skills: research, editing (organizing), copyediting, typing, proofreading. If your work experience does not include anything even remotely connected with editing, you might get unpaid experience as a volunteer on a local newspaper or an organization newsletter. Or you might turn to adult education.

FAMOUS EDITORS SCHOOLS

Courses in editorial skills range from home-study surveys of proofreading and copyediting to an intensive six-week session in publishing procedures, conducted each summer by Radcliffe College. And every university journalism department has courses in proofreading and such, some of which are offered to adult education students. They may be geared to newspaper and magazine work, but basic techniques are identical. Many of these courses are listed in *LMP*, along with programs in graphic arts and book production. Neither author of this book has taken any of these courses, so we cannot recommend or disparage any of them. Course catalogs may be obtained from any of the schools listed in Appendix III.

SETTING UP SHOP

Sooner or later, once you start freelancing, you will *have* to get organized. Do it sooner and prevent headaches. Chapter 7 explains how to set up tax records of business income and expenditures, as well as various types of business and personal insurance. You can begin freelancing at the kitchen table, but if you intend to take your work seriously, and if you want your family and friends to take you and it seriously, set up a work area. Your basic equipment should include a table or desk, a comfortable chair, a typewriter (for query letters, bills, indexes, style sheets), and access to a telephone. If you have to buy any of this equipment, save the receipts and depreciate the expense (pages 191–193) on your tax returns. You will also need pencils with erasable lead, nonerasable typing paper, stationery, a good desk dictionary, and a style manual. This is the minimum. In addition, specialized assignments may require specialized reference books or equipment. And you should have a clock nearby to remind you to keep track of your hours.

Good lighting is your most important equipment, for your eyes are your most important asset (in editorial work at least). Standard lighting recommended for study areas is a desk lamp of at least 200 watts plus an overhead (ceiling) light. Do not skimp on lighting! Try to work by indirect daylight if at all possible. Also, your desk top or blotter should have a matte finish. A shiny top will reflect light into your eyes (like snow glare on a bright winter day). A reading stand or board—like an artist's drawing board—can help relieve strain, for it is easier to read type if it is perpendicular to your line of sight. This also helps cut down on glare.

Eye specialists recommend hourly breaks of about five minutes. Rest your eyes and stretch your legs at the same time. To help rest your eyes during a break, cover them with your cupped palms so that your fingers cross on your forehead. If you "see" only black, then you are relaxed and your eyes are functioning normally. If spots, colors, shapes, or anything else appears, this indicates you are still straining. Rest your eyes—and your mind—until these intruders disappear. Or look into the distance, out a window, to flex your eye muscles after close work.

BILLING METHODS

The stickiest problem confronting new—and experienced—freelancers is billing. In 1973, questionnaires were sent to publishers asking what rates they paid, and to freelancers asking what rates they charged. The rates freelancers reported being paid tended to be higher than those the publishers quoted. For example, twenty-four of the copy editors earned $4.50 an hour or less, twenty charged $5 an hour, and twenty-eight charged even more, some as high as $10 an hour. Meanwhile, almost all of those publishers gracious enough to admit to rates quoted $4 to $5 an hour. Current publishers' rates in the New York area ran about $5 an hour for everything except proofreading (which averaged 50¢ an hour less), typing (paid by the page), and translating and writing (paid by the word).[1] The discrepancy between publishers' rates and freelancers' hourly earnings arises because many freelancers, regarding them-

[1] At publication of the revised edition, in 1979, rates have increased by about a dollar all around, but they are sure to go up again. Find out what the going rate is before you discuss money with a publisher.

selves as underpaid, charge what they feel the market will bear. How are their rates arrived at?

Standard working speeds are approximately seven to ten pages an hour for copyediting, four to six galleys an hour for proofreading, and five book pages an hour for indexing. Freelancers who work faster charge by the total job rather than by the hour. Thus a copy editor will submit a bill for forty to fifty-five hours work for a 400-page manuscript, whether or not the work actually took her that number of hours. Many freelancers, including the authors of this book and more than half of the freelancers responding to the questionnaire, acknowledge—some quite ruefully, some as a matter of fact—that they use this method in computing their bills.

Freelancers resort to this practice because of two inequities inherent in by-the-hour rates. First, the faster freelancers work, the quicker they finish an assignment, the less they get paid. "I'm extremely fast but accurate," one freelancer wrote. "However, I must accept the same (low) hourly rates paid to slower, less experienced workers. This means I would get paid *less* for doing a better job." Why does a publisher prefer to pay $4 per hour for fifteen hours rather than $6 per hour for ten hours? Only the bookkeeping department knows for sure.

The second inequity is that, ironically, some longtime freelancers earn less than beginners. They started working for a publisher when its rates were $3 or $4 an hour—and they continue to get that rate, even though newcomers ask for, or are just given, $5. Lack of communication among freelancers is one reason for this; the fear of not getting *any* work is another reason. As one freelancer put it, "Generally, freelancers are a poorly paid crew, and I gather that many publishers are still in the fiscal Dark Ages in their assessment of the value of services they perform." Amen.

If you do decide to bill by the total job, using the guidelines quoted here, keep track of your hours anyway. Maybe you are not working as fast as you think you are! A bit of psychology to ponder when deciding on the amount to bill: $200 on an invoice looks a lot steeper than $196.

"The Going Rate" feature in *Freelancer's Newsletter* may give you some idea of what to charge. The reported rates in that column were in the same ranges as those reported by freelancers responding to the survey done for this book.

Freelancers require no office space, insurance, workmen's compensation or Social Security payments, salaries when there is no work, vacations, or sick pay. Publishers should raise their hourly rates, or at least set page or line rates instead (so faster freelancers would not be handicapped). The current situation forces freelancers to pad their bills in order to make a living. As in any job, experience and expertise should bring higher wages.

HOT ON THE TRAIL

You have finished an assignment, as competently as you know how, and have sent the work and your bill back to the publisher and . . . Sometimes a profound silence ensues, leaving you to wonder if the

publisher (1) hated your work, (2) loved it but
thought you overcharged, or (3) just does not have
anything else for you to do right now. *Keep in touch.*
If you have not heard from the copy chief or production editor within a month, it certainly does not hurt
to call (or drop a postcard if you are out of town), say
hello, and ask if any new assignments are coming up
"so I can schedule my time." Quite a few freelancers
complain about lack of communication with the publisher, of feeling out of touch and isolated. "The only
way I ever learn about house style changes is by editing a manuscript in the previously acceptable manner and then getting a phone call complaining that
they don't do things that way anymore," one freelancer lamented. "Also, it is difficult for a freelancer
to know what her work is worth. We don't know what
other freelancers make, and we don't hear much
about the quality of our work. I figure I must do acceptable work because they keep sending manuscripts." You cannot do anything about the publisher
not calling you, but you can make the effort. There is
a delicate line between hounding an editor for assignments and keeping in touch. It is probably different for every editor and every freelancer; you will
just have to feel your way along.

Every six months or so (sooner if your assignments
start tapering off), send out another round of letters,
just so your resume stays near the top of the "current" pile. Every freelancer has had the experience
of getting an assignment solely because she happened to call or send a letter on a particular day.
Even if you get a steady but intermittent supply of
work from a firm, you should keep reminding the edi-

tors of your existence, or you may find yourself sup-
planted by more aggressive newcomers.

One of the pitfalls for freelancers, although it may
seem at first like a break, is taking an open-end temporary job, working exclusively for one publisher. In
such a job you may even go to work every day in the
company office, with all the headaches of regular
employment (commuting time and expense, regi-
mented work hours) and none of the benefits (vacations, sick pay). Meanwhile, your job sources at other
firms could dry up, so when your temporary assignment ends, you have to start all over again getting
acquainted.

FAR-OUT FREELANCERS

It is hard enough keeping in touch with a publisher when you are in the same town. If you live
some distance away, or if you cannot be reached during the day because of another job or whatever, the
problem is even greater. When you apply for an assignment in another town, assure the publisher you
will mail the work back so that it *reaches* them (not
leaves your house) the day it is due. For anything
you type—research, a style sheet, an index—save a
carbon. You may want to offer to photocopy your
work and save the copy until the publisher gives you
the all-clear.

For mailing materials such as manuscripts and galleys, the Post Office has a *Special Fourth Class Rate*,
but Fourth Class packages are sent the same as parcel
post: not too speedily. *Special Handling* will ensure
quicker delivery (the package will be treated as First

Class mail, and will be delivered at the first normal delivery time). *Special Delivery* results in even quicker service: The package is delivered within an hour after being received at the Post Office in the designated city.

The way you want the package mailed should be clearly marked on the outside wrapping, plus the magic word "Manuscript." A letter to the publisher can be enclosed; add appropriate First Class postage and note "Letter Enclosed" on the face of the package.

Whether or not you enclose a letter, be certain the publisher's name and address are *inside* the package as well as on the outside. Occasionally wrappings are torn, smeared, or completely lost. Take extra precautions in wrapping: Use reinforced wrapping tape *and* string. Or buy special book-mailing bags, which have an excelsior-stuffed lining and are stapled shut.

The publisher may ask you to return assignments First Class Special Delivery or Air Express, which are expensive. Rates vary by destination. (You can obtain a complete rate card from the Post Office.) If you do a lot of package mailing, get an accurate scale to weigh parcels at home so that you can include postage expense in your *enclosed* bill. Do *not* itemize this cost in your bill to the publisher; instead, add it into your hourly total. Just as you would charge the publisher for your time if you hand-delivered material, you should charge for having the Post Office deliver it (or a messenger service if you choose to use one).

If you work during the day and cannot be reached at your job, or if you are in and out on errands, it might pay to invest in an answering service or an answering service machine. Two serendipitous benefits: (1) If you are at home but are trying to concentrate, the machine or service answers your phone (some machines let you listen in to decide if you want to speak to the caller); (2) the machine can be set, or the service instructed, to say you are "working on a rush assignment" rather than away from your home, thus foiling potential thieves. To find a reliable answering service, ask a friend who's a doctor, an actor . . . or a freelancer.

Chapter 3

ENGLISH AS SHE IS RIT

THE author has committed to paper her precious thoughts. The editor has gone over the manuscript, rewriting or reorganizing if necessary and checking dates, facts, details. It is time for the copy editor to make her contribution.

Most books are copyedited. Sometimes the editor serves a dual role, but more often the manuscript is given to a professional copy editor—frequently a freelancer. Most of the major publishing companies in the United States use freelance copy editors. There is definitely work available, and it is interesting, challenging, and profitable.

Copy editors check manuscripts for correct grammar, punctuation, and spelling; make certain there is a consistent style; reword where needed; and at least question any inconsistency or suspected inaccuracy. They may also be called upon to do extensive research, rewriting, or reorganizing.

It is vital to bear in mind that a copy editor is not the counterpart of Miss Knopfel, your tenth-grade English teacher. Miss K. corrected compositions with a firm, inflexible hand. She was Authority; you were a neophyte come to learn at her feet. She taught that a sentence never started with "and" and never ended with a preposition—plus numerous other hard-and-fast rules. A composition that deviated from her teachings was red-penciled and graded down.

Copy editors are not out to correct the author in the manner of Miss Knopfel. Rather, their job is to enhance the author's prose and make it more readable. If misspellings occur in a book, many readers will be taken aback and are apt to lose faith in the author, even though what he has to say may be brilliant. Incorrect facts, wrongly attributed quotes, and garbled sentences have the same effect.

More obliquely, few readers will notice occasional stylistic inconsistencies: "ax" on page 12, "axe" on page 34; "traveled" on page 17, "travelled" on page 92; "thirty-three sheep" on page 21, "33 people" on page 99. But the sum total of such inconsistencies will give readers an uneasy feeling that something is wrong. They may not be able to pinpoint the irritants, but they are likely to become subconsciously upset—and may lose interest in the book.

Divided loyalties characterize copy editors. On one hand they are the best friend a reader has, for they lubricate the author's prose. Simultaneously, copy editors must get into the swing of the author's style, think with her and write with her, understand not only what she is saying but how she is saying it. Thomas Wolfe and Carson McCullers did not write about their hometowns in the same way. A copy editor must go along with individual styles. She would not make Wolfe's sentences succinct or merge Ernest Hemingway's clipped sentences to make them longer and more flowing. Until a copy editor becomes intimate with the author's way of writing, she can only do half the job: the more mechanical aspect of correcting spelling, inconsistencies, and such. Experienced copy editors can usually get in tune with an author after twenty pages or so; less experienced copy editors may have to zip through the entire book—before ever beginning to copyedit—in order to become the author's alter ego.

PROFILE OF A SUCCESSFUL COPY EDITOR

Basically, a copy editor must have a firm foundation in English usage, grammar and spelling, a well-rounded general background plus an awareness of current news, and an "ear" for the written word.

If the following faulty sentences offend you, you can consider yourself up on your English:

The entire group are going.[1]
She was born Febr. 7, 1939 in Brooklyn.[2]
After gulping three martinis, the room began to spin.[3]
The preceeding editor was harrassed.[4]

It is the rare student who paid close attention to grammar lessons in school. Copy editors—no matter how experienced—should periodically review a good English-grammar textbook so that unintentionally faulty construction can be pounced on and righted.

A copy editor's general knowledge can turn a good

[1] . . . group is going.
[2] . . . Feb. 7, 1939, in Brooklyn.
[3] Dangling modifier: The room did not imbibe.
[4] . . . preceding . . . harassed (not one author in a hundred spells these correctly).

book into a fine one. You have undoubtedly found factual errors in published books. If the author, editor, or copy editor had had your knowledge; the error would have been caught before publication. This is a gray area for a copy editor. She is not expected to research every fact, but she is supposed to look up or query anything that seems wrong. (First try to verify a suspicious fact; if you cannot find it, then query it.) The more the copy editor knows, the more she will be able to question. It is usually best to check the first few facts—dates, names, and similar information—in a manuscript. If these seem all right, you can feel more confident about the author's thoroughness and care. If there are discrepancies, check facts throughout the manuscript.

Seemingly incorrect facts should be brought to the author's attention but should *not* be changed by the copy editor; it is possible that the source books are wrong and the author correct. For example, a recent manuscript went on and on about Zane Grey's father, Mr. Gray. Turns out that Zane, in a fit of pique, changed the spelling of his last name.

Similarly, the wording, punctuation, and spelling of well-known quotations—such as those from the Bible, famous poems, historic documents—should also be verified for accuracy. But a copy editor should not try to check obscure quotes or facts unless specifically asked by the publisher to do such research. Also note that the copy editor should bring to the publisher's attention any statements that might be libelous.

A scientific book published by a distinguished company stated: "The explosion of Mont Pelée extinguished every spark of life on Krakatoa." Mont Pelée *did* explode and Krakatoa *was* devastated, but the events were separated by nineteen years and ten thousand miles. Some copy editors might immediately question the accuracy of the sentence because of their general knowledge. Others might come across the error in the course of verifying the spelling of Mont Pelée and Krakatoa. Both author and editor should have caught the blunder, but copy editors need to be alert for such goofs.

Even more upsetting are errors made by copy editors themselves. One freelancer carefully corrected "He was taken prisoner by the Bey of Algiers" to read ". . . the Bay of Algiers." Looking up unfamiliar words helps avoid such acute embarrassment.

A similar mistake, but slightly more esoteric, can occur with the words *whiskey* and *whisky*. The conscientious copy editor who selects one of these spellings as "style" after the author/editor has carefully distinguished between Scotch or Canadian *whisky* and all other *whiskey* is making a factual error. General knowledge is all that can help identify questionable statements or spellings.

Keeping abreast of current news is equally important for copy editors. New words keep entering the English language, new spellings slowly become preferred. For example, Bangladesh, formerly East Pakistan, exploded into the headlines in 1971. Most newspapers and magazines at first spelled it as two words: Bangla Desh. In a short while, however, *Bangladesh* became the preferred spelling. Similarly, Webster's prefers *bussing* (meaning to transport in a bus as well as to kiss). However, an Ivory-soap percentage of periodicals uses only one *s* for transportation: *busing* schoolchildren. A manuscript in which the spelling of this word goes along with the current trend should not be corrected to agree with Webster's; a manuscript that agrees with Webster's should probably be queried since it is out of step.

Country names change, and a book that uses an old-hat appellation will seem dated. Current almanacs and periodicals, especially U.N. publications and the *National Geographic*, are the best sources of information. (African nations are particularly subject to change.) Here are some renamings:

Basutoland *to* Lesotho
Bechuanaland *to* Botswana
British Guiana *to* Guyana
Ceylon *to* Sri Lanka
Democratic Republic of the Congo *to* Republic of Zaire
East Pakistan *to* Bangladesh
French Somaliland *to* French Territory of the Afars and
  Issas
Muscat and Oman *to* Oman
Northern Rhodesia *to* Zambia
Nyasaland *to* Malawi
Papua and New Guinea *to* Papua New Guinea
South West (Southwest) Africa *to* Namibia
Southern Rhodesia *to* Rhodesia
Spanish Guinea (Fernando Po and Río Muni) *to* Equatorial Guinea
Tanganyika and Zanzibar *to* Tanzania

And if you ever come across the land known as the Persian Gulf States/Trucial States/Union of Arab Emirates, sit back and take stock. This country's name changes almost yearly.

The third attribute of a successful copy editor is the ability to recognize a poorly written sentence, paragraph, chapter, or book. This is partly an innate sense and partly learned through exposure to good writing. A copy editor needs to know when a sentence should be reworded. "This day is fine" need not be changed to "This is a fine day." The author has written a clear, correct sentence; no need to tamper with it. However, the following examples leave much to be desired:

U.S. Marines were sent into the country to stabilize the conflict. [How do you stabilize conflict?]

Tara was the daughter of a fireman and a staunch Republican. [Who was the staunch GOPer—Tara, her father the fireman, or her mother?]

The data cover up until these countries ceased to exist by that name and also countries that were given aid at one time but are not any longer. [Gulp!]

A copy editor may—and should—correct a poorly written sentence or paragraph. Of course, an editor will occasionally specify only "stylistic" copy editing—no rewriting. In that case a copy editor can only point out horrendous paragraphs and pray that the editor or author will improve the prose. If a chapter or an entire book is poorly written, the copy editor should *not* rewrite or reorganize unless specifically given the green light to do so. Without such permission from the publisher, all the copy editor can do is inform the editor or the copyediting supervisor, and perhaps make brief notes outlining possible manuscript changes.

Infrequently an editor will give a copy editor carte blanche to improve the manuscript in any manner she sees fit. The trick in this situation is to know what to change. The copy editor must improve the author's manuscript, not write her own. "Creative" copyediting usually demands a double reading: once as a critic to revise and rewrite, and once purely as a copy editor.

Fiction and poetry, which are usually more stylized, should be copyedited with a much lighter hand than nonfiction or textbooks. Usually the publisher (editor, copyediting supervisor, or whoever) will ask that no major changes be made in fiction or poetry; suggested changes should be brought to the publisher's attention only on a tag attached to the manuscript or in a separate letter.

BECOMING A COPY EDITOR

The simplest, easiest way to become a freelance copy editor is to start off as an editorial employee of a publishing house, where you get on-the-job training. College-level courses involving some practical experience are also helpful (see Appendix III). Without someone to constructively criticize your work, it is difficult to learn the full range of a copy editor's responsibilities, to get a "feel" for the job. As a novice you might be able to get a few manuscripts, but it would be highly unusual to avoid making some sins of omission and commission. And these could kill your chances of future work. If you can get an experienced copy editor to review your initial efforts, this will be a great advantage. Criticism is hard to take, but it will be invaluable.

The best path to becoming a freelance copy editor, short of practical experience, is to obtain work first as a freelance proofreader (see Chapter 4) or typist for a publisher (see Chapter 6). As a proofreader you will be working with a copyedited manuscript. As a typist you may have a copyedited manuscript; it will probably be an edited one. You will see changes that have been made, suggested changes that have not been made, questions that have been asked, copyediting symbols. With this background, plus what you learn from this chapter, you will be able to branch into freelance copyediting and do a competent, respectable job that should earn you repeat assignments.

It is a fact of life that most copyediting supervisors—those who usually give out freelancing—are not apt to have the time to coach you in basics. These you must learn on your own. (It is also just as well not to broadcast that you are starting out. Have confidence in yourself. Unless you let on that you are new to the game, it probably will not be apparent.)

In applying to a publisher to become a freelance copy editor, you should send a complete resume (see Chapter 2), including any special skills or knowledge (superb plumber, sports fanatic, bridge expert, good knowledge of French). List your publishing experience, if any.

Some publishers require that applicants take a copyediting test, usually a take-at-home variety. The test will be chock-full of misspellings, style points, and inaccuracies to really put you through the mill. It is not uncommon to have someone else go over the test if you desire; the tests are so loaded with errors that you are bound to miss a point or two that you would probably catch in the course of copyediting a normal manuscript. (See Appendix IV for sample copyediting tests for you to practice with.)

When copyediting your first manuscripts, proceed slowly and deliberately. Look up style points and rules of grammar in a style manual, spelling in a dictionary, and so on. Be extra thorough. Maybe you will do only three or four pages an hour. But you will be building that proverbial good foundation. After you have checked the style manual umpteen times for when and how to use such things as an en dash, or italics versus quotes, the rule will become almost automatic; look it up a few more times until you are absolutely confident. Do this with each specific point. No matter how experienced a copy editor may be, there is always some new problem—or many of them—in every manuscript.

STYLE SHEETS

Few freelancers have photographic memories. Thus a copy editor should compile a style sheet for each manuscript, listing the decisions made concerning the main elements of style. If there are many proper nouns, a separate style sheet may be necessary for names and/or places. Words per se are usually alphabetized by initial letter on the style sheet; all the other style elements should be grouped, with punctuation style listed in one place, number style listed in another, and so on.

The proofreader refers to the copy editor's style sheet, so it must be neat and readable. Usually the working style sheet needs to be rewritten or typed. And the style sheet must be complete, so that the proofreader will know right from the start what style is being used.

On the following page is a sample style sheet—supposedly for a lengthy book—and a paragraph in accordance with it.

A worthwhile procedure is to jot down page numbers the first few times a stylistic point occurs. The author may use the spelling *advisor* on pages 2 and 13, then switch to *adviser* on page 27. At this point the copy editor would start paying close attention every time the word came up. Perhaps *-or* will only occur twice, and the rest of the manuscript will consistently be *-er*. Then the copy editor will set *-er* as the style and go back and find *advisor;* listing the initial page numbers simplifies the search. (Once the style is definitely set, the page numbers are no longer needed.)

Sooner or later the copy editor must reach a stylistic decision on every point that arises. If the author consistently uses one style at the beginning of a book, it is safe to set this as the style for the whole book. If his style suddenly changes along about page 400, the copy editor should just continue with the previously established style. Authors are not allowed to change their style in midstream. Assuming no general guidelines from the author or publisher, the copy editor sets the style based on the first pages of a manuscript—usually a maximum of the first 100 pages in a long book, fewer in a shorter manuscript.

POLITICS IS POKER: A. F. House

Series comma

No comma after short introductory phrase

Abbreviate states following cities

1972-73

one fourth

27%

1400 (no comma)

adviser	ghettos	President (of U.S.)
=age	handfuls	senators
attorney generals	jack-in-the-boxes	=size
chairman (particular one)	leaped	toward
cigaret	naive	VFW hall
descendant	OK	
fulfill	Pa.	
gaveling	phony	

During the 1972-73 campaign a candidate for President was
speaking at the VFW hall in Lincoln, Pa. Other dignitaries
present included attorney generals, government advisers,
senators, company presidents. The middle-age, small-size
chairman kept gaveling the 1440-man audience to quiet handfuls of hecklers. About one fourth of those in attendance--
actually 27%--thought the candidate was a phony, although
he was a descendant of immigrants who had lived in ghettos.
The naive candidate continued speaking. Suddenly two cigaret=
smoking men leaped up like jack-in-the-boxes. "Tell us all
you know," one yelled. "It won't take long." The candidate
turned: "OK, I'll fulfill your request and reveal all we
both know. It won't take any longer."

STYLE MANUALS

The copy editor must know the elements that comprise style so that she can make decisions. But what is the basis for the decisionmaking? A dictionary—usually Webster's—is used for spelling. A style manual is used for the other points.

There are two premiere style books: *Words into Type* (Appleton-Century-Crofts, New York, 1974) and *A Manual of Style* (University of Chicago Press, Chicago, 1969). The former will herein be abbreviated WIT; the latter is generally called Chicago.

In addition to these two manuals, publishers may have a house style, which takes precedence over style manuals. However, house style sheets usually give a handful of publisher preferences and then dictate "follow *Words into Type*" or "follow *Chicago Style Manual*." There are other published style manuals—including *The New York Times Style Book* and the *Government Printing Office Style Manual*—but they are not as widely used.

WIT and Chicago cover the whole spectrum of publishing, from dotting *i*'s through grammar to setting a book in type. A copy editor must be thoroughly familiar with at least one of these manuals. This does *not* mean memorizing the style manual; it does mean being aware of what is in the book and looking up a particular point when it occurs in a manuscript. Is *Rev. Jones* accepted form? Is *from 1962–67* allowable, or should it be *from 1962 to 1967*? Should *a priori* be set in italics? Are quotes used when someone is thinking aloud? What's the Roman numeral for 800?

A copy editor should be sufficiently familiar with WIT or Chicago to realize that answers to these questions—and thousands more—are somewhere in the style manual. Then it is just a matter of looking in the index to find where it is explained and coming up with the answer.

Both WIT and Chicago are necessities for every copy editor; they are not interchangeable. Publishers may specifically request that one or the other be used. (One note in passing: WIT has a more complete index, which makes it easier to quickly locate a specific point.)

In copyediting a rather technical book, the copy editor may be helped by referring to a special dictionary of appropriate technical terms—for example, *Chambers's Technical Dictionary* or *The International Encyclopedia of Cooking*. It is also valuable to have an encyclopedia available to check names and dates.

An already published book on the same subject as the manuscript at hand may also be helpful. In working with a book on antiques, for example, the copy editor may want to refer to a well-known book on that subject to check spellings, see what words are italicized, verify dates and periods. It is not necessary to mimic the style of the printed book, but it can serve as a general guide. For a sports book the copy editor should refer to a directory put out by the sports league or governing body in order to check such items as player and team name spellings, dates, scores of games.

STYLE

The crux of copyediting is styling a manuscript: choosing between alternatives that are equally acceptable, equally "right." There are six major elements involved in the all-inclusive term "style": punctuation; capitalization; abbreviations; spelling; numbers; and special display matter (footnotes, tables, lists, extracts, bibliography). A copy editor must identify the style to be followed in a particular manuscript, then list her decisions on the style sheet. The following nonsensical paragraph is an example of two alternate styles, both perfectly acceptable.

July 1967 (*July, 1967,*) was a (*an*) historic month for 20 (*twenty*) astronauts, for LBJ's administration (*L.B.J.'s Administration*) approved plans for traveling (*travelling*) outside earth's (*Earth's*) atmosphere. Some 1500 (*1,500*) astronauts, advisers (*advisors,*) and technicians had got (*gotten*) over cooperation (*coöperation, co-operation*) difficulties and had reexamined (*re-examined*) priorities. The World Health Organization suggested splashdown (*splash-down*) near archipelagos (*archipelagoes*), but the organization's (*Organization's*) ideas were not 100% (*one hundred percent, 100 percent, one hundred per cent, 100 per cent*) acceptable.

The style in each phrase differs, but each clearly relays its message. Readers would comprehend, no matter which version they read. The copy editor's task is to determine the style to be used throughout the entire book, and then make certain it is followed exactly, precisely, minutely, page after page. Such consistency gives a book cohesiveness so that readers can concentrate on what the author is saying.

Some authors write with a consistent style. If they choose the spelling *adviser* on page 2, they do not write *advisor* on page 92. If they choose to use *15%*, they do not do an about-face later on and write out *fifteen percent*. But such authors are rare birds. The editor may pick up stylistic inconsistencies and correct them in the manuscript, but editors are usually more concerned with content and readability. Therefore it becomes a primary duty of the copy editor to identify the style used by the author and to be certain it is followed throughout the entire manuscript. If the author is not consistent, the copy editor must ascertain which style to use and then change the manuscript accordingly.

The publisher may provide style guidelines (a house style sheet). This becomes the bible, and the copy editor must see to it that the manuscript follows the style she has been instructed to use. Only in cases in which the author is inconsistent and the publisher gives no directions can the copy editor follow the dictates of her own mind. A copy editor may abhor *meager* and get an inordinate charge out of *meagre*. But if the author has consistently used *-er* or the house style calls for *-er*, the copy editor must suppress her personal preference.

A copy editor needs to know all the elements that make up style so that she can identify them. If a copy editor does not realize that both *meager* and *meagre* are correct but alternate spellings, she is not likely to notice the word the first time it pops up in a manuscript. Either option looks fine. And when this word appears later, she will probably overlook it again. Then it will be a matter of chance whether it has been spelled the same way. She should decide which spelling to use and write it down on a style sheet.

This same risk holds true for all of the six major elements of style. The copy editor pinpoints alternatives, chooses (or is told) which style to follow, keeps a record of the choices (her style sheet), and makes the manuscript consistent.

The following sections discuss the style points that arise most frequently in all types of manuscripts. This is by no means a complete rundown of style alternatives. Tomes are available on style (see Appendix II), which include everything from putting a period at the end of a sentence—something a copy editor should not have to be told—to the most obscure style point that may crop up once in every thousand manuscripts. However, before a copy editor can use a style manual or a house style sheet, or even make up her own style to follow, she must be aware of, and alert to the six major style elements.

PUNCTUATION

The most basic style point is the series comma (also called the serial or Harvard comma), used before a conjunction connecting three or more elements:

Dick, Gordon, and Gene   Dick, Gordon and Gene

As with all elements of style, using or omitting the series comma is purely the choice of the author/publisher/copy editor. If this comma is used, it must appear consistently. If it is not used, it should be omitted consistently—*except* where its absence creates ambiguity:

A sundae is made with ice cream, syrup and nuts if desired.

Fresh sheets, the smell of breakfast and Mom remind me of home.

In these examples there is a chance the reader could become confused because of the absence of the series comma. The comma should therefore be inserted *even if the general style calls for no series comma:* "ice cream, syrup, and nuts if desired" and "fresh sheets, the smell of breakfast, and Mom . . ."

It is also a point of style whether a comma will be used after a short introductory adverbial phrase or clause:

In May she met her man.   In June, she married him.

Again, either style is perfectly correct; just be consistent. Of course, an exception must be made if omitting this comma produces an unclear sentence:

When the branch breaks down we'll go.
If canvas shows you are pulling stitches too tight.

The introductory comma should be omitted only after a *short* phrase or clause. Five, six, or seven words is usually set as the arbitrary maximum (again, this is style). A long introductory adverbial phrase or clause needs a comma in order to give readers a pause to catch their breath.

One additional punctuation style point occurs frequently. A comma following *thus, hence, accordingly, consequently,* and *yet* at the beginning of a sentence is optional:

Thus we decided to go dancing.   Hence, he got a tux.

The present trend is to use a minimum number of commas. It is more popular *not* to use the series comma, *not* to use a comma after a short introductory phrase or clause, *not* to use a comma following "thus" and similar introductory words.

These are the most basic punctuation *style* points. There are myriad other rules regarding punctuation, which can be checked in a style manual when and if a question arises.

CAPITALIZATION

There are two styles of capitalization: an Up Style (capitalizing the first letter of many words) and a down style (lowercasing the first letter of words if there is a choice). For example:

Queen Mary/the Queen of England (Up Style)
Mayor Doe/the mayor of Sheboygan (down style)
Fox Theater/the Theater (Up Style)
Central Park/the park (down style)
the National League/the League (Up Style)
the Defense Department/the department (down style)
the Roman Empire/the Empire (Up Style)
New York City/the city of New York (down style)

A general style should be set for a book: either an Up Style or a down style. Then only *exceptions* need be noted. For instance, in a book with a generally down style, the author/publisher/copy editor might choose to always capitalize[5] words referring to the President of the United States but lowercase presidents of other countries:

The President left his office in the White House to meet the president·of Mexico.

Note that in both up and down styles, nouns that may be capitalized when part of a specific name are lowercased when used collectively:

the Fox Theater/the Fox and Bijou theaters
the Hudson River/the Hudson and Ramapo rivers

In titles of books, chapters, poems, periodicals, lectures, and the like, the initial letter of each important word should be capitalized. Articles (*a, an, the*) and coordinate conjunctions are not capitalized, unless they are the first word. Prepositions of five or more letters are usually capped, and four-letter prepositions may be capped; this is a matter of style.

News *F*rom Home   Living *w*ith Mary
A Letter *t*o Joe   The Heavens *A*bove Us

But: Prepositions that are an integral part of the verb are always capped:

Mother Drops *I*n   Lovers Break *O*ff Relationship

[5] "Capitalize" means to capitalize the *first letter* of the word, not the whole word. "Full caps" signifies that every letter of the word is to be uppercased.

In infinitives, *to* is not capitalized in a title unless it is the first word:

Waiting to Go Home   Dying to See Old Shep

After a hyphen in a title, it is a matter of style whether to capitalize the first letter:

The Able-Bodied Seaman   The Pot-bellied Statesman
The Twenty-One Survivors   One-fifth Pass Exams

There are a few more important points concerning capitalization style:
SMALL CAPS should be used for A.M., P.M., B.C., A.D.
Negro and *Caucasian* are always capped; *blacks* and *whites*, plus any slang words for the races, are usually lowercased.
A full sentence following a colon may begin with a capital or a lowercase letter. This is a frequently occurring style point.

There are two choices: He can work or starve.
He has two options: he can drop in or drop out.

ABBREVIATIONS
The copy editor must decide whether periods will be used with abbreviations: UN or U.N.? USSR or U.S.S.R.? YMCA or Y.M.C.A.? There are three possible styles: Use periods all of the time, some of the time, none of the time.
The latter choice is becoming increasingly popular because of the modern tendency to omit punctuation wherever possible. Rarely are periods used in all abbreviations.

The most common general procedure at present is to omit periods *if the abbreviation is pronounced as a word:* NATO, UNICEF, WACS, CARE, CORE. Otherwise, periods are used: U.N., U.S.S.R., R.F.D., Y.M.C.A., A.F.L.–C.I.O., f.o.b., C.I.A., C.B.S., A. & P.

Months of the year may be abbreviated if given with a full date: Sept. 21, 1973. Similarly, titles may be abbreviated if used with the person's full name: Col. John Glenn, Gov. Ronald Reagan, Rev. Jonathan Evans. This is a matter of style. However, in books it is considered poor usage—*not* a stylistic choice—to abbreviate months or titles if not given in full. (Such abbreviating is done in newspapers and some periodicals.) Therefore, unless specifically instructed otherwise, a copy editor should use *September 21* rather than *Sept. 21; Colonel Glenn* rather than *Col. Glenn.*

The copy editor must also decide whether states are to be abbreviated or written out when accompanied by city names: *Newark, New Jersey,* or *Newark, N.J.* And note that there are alternate abbreviations for a few states: Calif. *or* Cal.; Kans. *or* Kan.; Nebr. *or* Neb.; N. Mex. *or* N.M.; N. Dak. (S. Dak.) *or* N.D. (S.D.); Oreg. *or* Ore.; Penn. *or* Pa.; Wisc. *or* Wis. States with less than six letters are usually not abbreviated: Idaho, Iowa, Maine, Ohio, Texas, Utah. Alaska is usually not abbreviated because Alabama has prior claim on *Ala.;* however, *Alas.* can be used. There are also two-letter abbreviations for each state, promulgated by the Post Office. These are not yet in general book use.

One recurring problem with abbreviations concerns space between the letters when periods are used. The initials of a person's name are usually spaced: O. H. Palmer. States (and "U.S.") can be spaced (N. J.) or not spaced (N.J.); the latter is more common. Most other abbreviations are usually "set tight"—set without space between the letters.

SPELLING

Though Miss Knopfel back in tenth–grade English class might be the last to admit it, our language is in flux. One of the most far-reaching "fluxes" occurred in 1965 when *Webster's Third New International Dictionary* was released. The dictionary editors chose to make some major stylistic and other changes. These included omitting hyphens after almost all prefixes. Thus

reenact	*not* re-enact
preempt	*not* pre-empt
cooperate	*not* co-operate

And so on and so on. There was a short-lived—but vehement—protest. Some publishers decided to go along with the omitted hyphen only in words in which the last letter of the prefix was not the same as the first letter of the stem word; that is, accept *reclassify* but hyphenate *re-elect.* (*The American Heritage Dictionary* still prefers the hyphen in this instance.) A few publishers vowed to cling to Webster's Second and ignore the new edition.

Nowadays the uproar has quieted and Webster's Third has become the standard, the authority, for just about every publisher. (Webster's Third is the unabridged dictionary and *Webster's Seventh New Collegiate Dictionary* is the abridged version.) There are numerous other dictionaries, each with particular strong points. But Webster's Third/Seventh is the ultimate source for almost all publishing houses. Remember, however, that new editions appear frequently: always ask which edition of which dictionary is preferred.

Word spellings vary slightly among the latest editions of different dictionaries. For example:

Webster's	Funk & Wagnalls	Random House	American Heritage
X ray (noun)	X-ray	x-ray (*also* X-ray)	x ray (*also* X ray)
puree	purée	purée	purée
copyboy	copy boy	copyboy	copy boy
Vietminh	Viet Minh	Vietminh (*also* Viet Minh)	Vietminh (*also* Viet Minh)

Thus dictionaries vary—not often, but frequently enough so that a conscientious copy editor cannot "get by" using a dictionary other than Webster's if the publisher specifies Webster spelling.

The compounding of words is one of the most rapidly changing areas of style. Many words once hyphenated or written as two words are now "set tight"—spelled as one word. *Moneymaking* and *breakthrough* are two common examples, as well as words with prefixes. (British spelling uses many more hyphens: dining-room, meeting-place, etc.) And note that spelled-out fractions are usually not hyphenated these days: one fourth, two thirds.

Dictionaries choose their spellings based on "current usage." In passing, it is interesting to note words such as *good-bye* (*good-by*) and *re-create* (to create anew). Webster's, Funk & Wagnalls, Random House, and American Heritage dictionaries give these spell-

ings. However, check current periodicals. *Goodbye*
(*goodby*) and *recreate* are frequently seen in print.
(*Re-lease*, meaning to lease again, retains its
hyphen—so far.) The next editions of these dictionaries are likely to reflect such changes.

Of course, it has never been claimed that English
is a consistent language. Witness these aberrations
from Webster's:

girl friend/boyfriend
tote board/blackboard
window box/windowsill
half crown, half eagle/half-dollar/halfpenny
lifeboat, lifeguard/life belt, life raft/life-force
shortcake/sponge cake, pound cake

And then there are *copy editor* and *copyediting*.
Dictionaries give *copy editor* (but *copyreader* and
copywriter). The American Heritage and Random
House dictionaries give *copy-edit* for the verb; *A
Manual of Style* published by the University of Chicago prefers *copy edit;* Webster's omits the word. But
since *proofreading* is one word, the authors of this
book have opted for *copyediting* while going with
copy editor. And this book arbitrarily uses *freelancer*
and *freelancing*, based on common spelling in publishing circles.

Since compound-word style is changing so fast, it
is advisable to check all compounds in an up-to-date
dictionary. Also be alert to style changes while reading respected newspapers, periodicals, and books.

Dictionaries give alternate spellings if both are
common usage. There are two types: (1) inter-

changeable alternates, such as *ax* and *axe*, and (2) preferred spelling versus variants, such as *omelet* and *omelette*.

Webster's identifies interchangeable spellings by separating them with the word *or*. This indicates that *neither spelling is preferred*, no matter which is listed first.[6] For example:

caddie *or* caddy   luster *or* lustre

Based on Webster's, either spelling would be perfectly acceptable.

Variant spellings are indicated in Webster's by the word *also* (instead of *or*). Thus

woolly *also* wooly

shows that Webster's prefers the double *l* but wants the world to know that a single *l* is acceptable, although less frequently used. Standard variants may also be entered separately in Webster's if their alphabetical position is more than one column away from the main entry. Thus

loth *var of* loath

is equivalent to the entry

loath *also* loth

Again, *loath* is preferred, but *loth* is acceptable.

Other dictionaries follow basically the same proce-

[6] There is a minor hedge: If the words separated by *or* are not in alphabetical order (plow *or* plough; guerrilla *or* guerilla), the first is "slightly more common but not common enough to justify calling them unequal."

dure. The front matter in any dictionary explains the method employed. A copy editor needs to know when spellings are interchangeable and when one is a variant. As an example, an author might alternate between *ax* and *axe*. According to Webster's, these are interchangeable spellings (Funk & Wagnalls gives *axe* to the British), so the copy editor would arbitrarily decide which to use. However, if an author used *loath* half of the time and *loth* the rest of the time, the copy editor should use *loath* since this is the preferred spelling and *loth* is a variant. If the author consistently uses an acceptable but obscure variant, the copy editor should check with the editor before changing it.

To make a manuscript consistent, copy editors must be able to identify words that have alternate spellings. It is nerve-wracking to come across a certain spelling on page 84 of a manuscript and to feel certain a different spelling was used earlier in the book. But where was it? If the earlier spelling has not been noted by the copy editor on her style sheet, she must now reread eighty-four pages to find the word.

Words that have alternate spellings fall into four categories: alternate plurals; alternate endings to verbs; alternate diacritic marks; and that infamous general category, "all other." There is not enough room in this entire book to give all such words, but the following lists, based on Webster's spellings (and in the order given in Webster's), are a starter and a reminder. *It is not a matter of which is preferred; rather, the copy editor must be aware of these alternates so that she can make the manuscript internally consistent.*

First are words with alternate plurals:

SINGULAR	PLURALS
apex	apexes, apices
appendix	appendixes, appendices
attorney general	attorneys general, attorney generals
beau	beaux, beaus
desperado	desperadoes, desperados
hoof	hooves, hoofs
jack-in-the-box	jack-in-the-boxes, jacks-in-the-box
maestro	maestros, maestri
no	noes, nos
phalanx	phalanxes, phalanges
tablespoonful	tablespoonfuls, tablespoonsful

Note that the plurals of some words are not a matter of style. Instead, they refer to different meanings of the word: indexes (of a book) but indices (mathematical signs); brothers (siblings) but brethren (society members).

In addition, the plurals of some words can be either the same as the singulars or can be plural endings. (Many of these are animals. The regular *s* or *es* ending—fishes—is often technically preferred for more than one species or kind.) Plurals are listed here in the order given in Webster's. Again, it is necessary to be aware of these alternates in order to make the manuscript internally consistent; either plural is "right" in many cases.

SINGULAR	PLURALS
Eskimo	Eskimo, Eskimos
fish	fish, fishes
fox	foxes, fox
gladiolus	gladioli, gladiolus, gladioluses

killdeer	killdeers, killdeer [7]
mackerel	mackerel, mackerels
nexus	nexuses, nexus
rhinoceros	rhinoceroses, rhinoceros, rhinoceri

A second category of alternate spellings, which the copy editor needs to note in order to make the manuscript consistent, is alternate endings to verbs. This occurs most frequently with words ending in *l*, such as *labeled/labelled, labeling/labelling*. Likewise, *dishevel, frivol, gambol, gavel, imperil, level, libel, marshal, marvel, model, travel*, and so on. However, verbs ending in *l* that have the accent on the last syllable can only be written with a double *l: compel, control, impel, rebel, repel*, etc.

Similarly, verbs ending with a *p* may offer the alternative of a single or a double *p: kidnaped/kidnapped, kidnaping/kidnapping, kidnaper/kidnapper. Hiccup* and *worship* are two more examples. And then there is *benefited/benefitted, benefiting/benefitting* or *diagramed/diagrammed, diagraming/diagramming*.

Irregular verbs also have to be watched: *got/gotten, leaped/leapt, lighted/lit, mowed/mown, proved/proven, quit/quitted*, and the like. And watch such words as *clueing/cluing, eyeing/eying, sautéed/sautéd*. A copy editor gets paid her money to make her choice.

Just a reminder: The preceding examples, and the following ones, are given so that the copy editor will be alert to *alternatives*, both of which may appear in a manuscript and which should be made consistent.

[7] But more than one deer are only *deer*.

The third category of alternate spellings is English-language words with diacritic marks. Among the most common are:

café, cafe
führer, fuehrer
naïveté, naiveté

entrée, entree
matériel, materiel
résumé, resume

The final category of alternate spellings, the "all other" group, is huge. Here are a select few.

adviser, advisor
Bern, Berne
  (Switzerland)
catercorner, kitty-corner
collectible, collectable
coquet, coquette
dexterous, dextrous
employee, employe
flier, flyer
fulfill, fulfil
guerrilla, guerilla
king-size, king-sized [8]
lady's slipper, lady slipper
lollipop, lollypop
Magna Charta, Magna Carta
Mojave, Mohave (desert)
Nazism, Naziism
OK, okay, o.k.
Romania, Rumania, Roumania
toward, towards [9]

ax, axe
Bighorn, Big Horn
  (U.S. river)
catsup, ketchup
cookie, cooky
crummy, crumby
dumbfound, dumfound
endways, endwise
frankfurt(er), frankfort(er)
golliwog, golliwogg
Hanukkah, Chanukah
klieg light, kleig light
likable, likeable
louver, louvre
marihuana, marijuana
moneyed, monied
nosy, nosey
phony, phoney
sizable, sizeable
yogurt, yoghurt

In dealing with each group of these spelling alternatives, a copy editor should try to be as consistent as

---

[8] The ending -size or -sized is always a matter of style.

[9] This word occurs in almost every book, so a copy editor must constantly be alert for it. "Toward" is usually preferred by publishers.

possible in styling groups of similar words. If *desperados* is the selected plural, then *ghettos*—not *ghettoes*—should also be the plural. If trave*l*ing is used, leve*l*ed and kidna*p*ed and benefi*t*ed should be used; if *entrée*, then *soirée*.

British Spellings

American publishers frequently want British spellings and words changed to their New World counterparts. Britishisms include:

1) The double *l* in verbs ending with *l:* libeller, marvelling, travelled.
2) The ending *our* in words where Americans use only *or:* behaviour, colour, favour, honour, neighbour, rumour.
3) An *s* where U.S. English uses a *z:* analyse, civilisation, cosy, hypnotise.
4) A *c* where U.S. English uses an *s:* offence, pretence.
5) The *t* ending for the past tense of verbs: dreamt (not dreamed), learnt, spelt.
6) Many more hyphens: dining-room, meeting-place.
7) *Mr* or *Mrs* without final periods.
8) Single quotation marks where Americans use double marks, and vice versa: 'Are you staying?' she asked. She then recounted, 'He said, "I will not go!"'
9) Punctuation marks outside quote marks when they are not part of the quotation: 'I guess I will not go', moaned Joe.
10) The ending *re* rather than *er:* centre, reconnoitre, theatre.

British words that may have to be Americanized include: biscuit (cracker), bonnet (hood) of a car, chips (French-fried potatoes), connexion (connection), draughts/drafts (checkers), ironmonger (hardware dealer), kerb (curb), lift (elevator), lorry (truck), nappy (diaper), petrol (gasoline), pram (baby carriage), scones (biscuits), sweets (candy), telly (television), tram (streetcar), tin (can), waggon (wagon), zip (zipper). Keep your pecker up (keep up your courage)!

NUMBERS

Numbers can be handled in three ways: Write them out as words, use figures, write some as words and some as figures. Newspaper style usually calls for numbers under ten to be written out. Book style varies, but probably the most common procedure is to write out numbers under 100 and use figures for all others. An extension of this latter style is to write out numbers under 100 *and* all round numbers over 100: six, six thousand, six million; but 620, 6200, 62,000,000 (or, more frequently, 62 million—easier than counting up all the zeroes).

The primary reason for using figures is to save space. *Twenty-three* versus *23; two thousand four hundred and forty-eight* versus *2448* (or *2,448;* the comma in thousands is also a matter of style). Another reason for using figures is the ease with which a reader can grasp the import: *93 casualties* is easier to comprehend—and makes more of an impact—than using words alone. The main rationale for *not* using figures is an aesthetic one. Numbers tend to stand out and make a choppy-looking page. (Lots of percent symbols, em dashes, italics, and the like have the same effect on a page.) In addition, too many numbers may make even light reading look ponderous. Thus most book publishers follow the write-out-under-100 rule.

There are exceptions where figures may be used. *Words into Type* and *A Manual of Style* go into great detail, with each style book varying somewhat. The following list gives examples of written-out numbers versus figures.

1) With A.M. or P.M., figures are used: 4 P.M., 11 A.M. Figures are also usually used with hours and minutes (*except* the half hour): 6:35, 12:20, eleven thirty. However: four o'clock, eleven in the morning.

2) In percents, figures are used with the percent symbol: 3%, 10%. If "percent" is written out as a word, figures may be used (a matter of style).

3) With dimensions and height, figures may be used: 4-inch board, 17-pound catfish, 5 feet tall. Figures are usually used with symbols: 4" x 3".

4) In a series where all elements refer to the same thing, figures are used if *one or more* elements in the series requires figures: 3 cheetahs, 17 aardvarks, 132 squirrels. However, not all figures occurring in a single sentence are in series: There are 3 cheetahs and 132 squirrels in the nation's seventy zoos. (Cheetahs and squirrels are a series, but zoos are not similar elements.)

5) Monetary amounts are usually written as figures if a symbol is used with them: $6, $6 million, £15.

6) Centuries are often given as figures: 14th cen-

tury, 2nd (2d) century. (Note 2nd *or* 2d; 3rd *or* 3d; 23rd *or* 23d, etc.)

7) Page numbers are always given as figures: pages 36–38. (Note full page numbers are usually given under 100: pages 41–43, *not* 41–3. However, over 100 the style may be 126–128, 126–28, or 126–8.)

8) Mixed numbers and decimals are almost always set as figures: 3⅓, 6.5.

9) Temperature and latitude and longitude are frequently figures: 45 degrees (45°); latitude 20 degrees W. (*or* west). (Note "F." for Fahrenheit or "C." for Centigrade may be spaced after the number and degree symbol (45° F.) or may be set tight (45°C.).

10) Miscellaneous numbers such as scores and years are usually figures: the Mets won 10–1; Mount Vesuvius erupted in 79 A.D.

Publishers frequently do not want figures used in the following instances, no matter what the cutoff rule is:

1) Numbers at the beginning of a sentence (variance from this rule is highly exceptional). Thus the sentence "1967 was a good year" should be reworded, perhaps "The year 1967 was a good one." The sentence "33 women protested" could be changed to "Thirty-three women protested" or "Some 33 women protested." (In case of emergency, "some" before the number usually helps.)

2) Similarly, publishers may prefer that a figure not end a sentence.

3) Some publishers want the number *one* written out in all cases (it is not as readily comprehended in context as other figures).

4) If two numbers come together, the first is usually written out: There were sixteen [*not* 16] 12-inch guns.

Two random notes: a particular century used as an adjective is usually not hyphenated if the word "century" is capped, but it is commonly hyphenated if that word is lowercased (to capitalize or not is style): 2nd Century fresco; 17th-century manuscript. Also, decades can be written in numerals with or without an apostrophe: 1930's or 1930s. 'Tis style.

SPECIAL DISPLAY MATTER

Footnotes, tables, lists, extracts, and bibliography are first copyedited just like regular textual matter. The copy editor must watch for factual accuracy, styling consistent with the entire manuscript, and general readability. But there is also a second phase: All must be carefully gone over en masse for consistency. For example, the first footnote may be typed with a paragraph indent, the second without this indent. Or one table may be labeled "Table I" and the next "Table 2." This second phase of copyediting special display matter is commonly done as a separate operation after the text itself has been copyedited.

Footnotes

There are two ways to identify footnotes: by numeral superscripts—[1], [2], etc.—or by standard symbols. In order of use, standard symbols are: * (asterisk); † (dagger); ‡ (double dagger); § (section mark); // (parallels); # (number sign); and then two of each, in the same order, if more symbols are needed.

Symbols are usually used only if there are very few

footnotes in the entire book. Numeral or symbol may occur within a sentence or at the end of a sentence. They should be set after all punctuation *except* before a semicolon (*Words into Type* style) or before a dash (Chicago Manual style).

The actual footnote may be typed directly below the footnoted material or at the bottom of the same page. Or footnotes may be grouped at the end of a chapter or at the back of the book. If they are typed individually as they occur, the copy editor should bracket the footnote and make a marginal note to the compositor: "footnote" or "ftn." enclosed in a circle. (Words enclosed in a circle indicate directions: compositors are instructed not to set in type anything that appears in a circle in the margin.)

The copy editor should make absolutely certain that footnotes are consecutive. Usually they are numbered chapter by chapter (footnotes 1 through 12 in Chapter I, footnotes 1 through 9 in Chapter II, etc.). Or they may run consecutively through the entire book. Rarely, they will be numbered per individual page; this is difficult since a typed manuscript page usually does not correspond to the printed page.

In addition:

1) Be certain all footnotes begin with paragraph indent or no paragraph indent (flush left).

2) Doublecheck all *ibid.*, *op. cit.*, and *loc. cit.* references to be certain there is a previous entry.

3) Make sure page references are styled consistently. These may be "pages 212–213," "pages 212–13," "pages 212–3," "pp. 212–213," and so on.

4) Doublecheck author's names and book titles

against information given in the text and/or bibliography.

Tables

First make certain that table headings follow a consistent style. Possible styles include (1) period, colon,
or em space following table numbers; (2) no final
punctuation after table title, or a final period; (3)
table number centered on a line alone or run in with
the title. Any combination is possible.

Also check column headings. Heads that run two
lines or more should be aligned either at the top or at
the bottom:

Number of Participants	Sex	Number of Participants	Sex

Rules (publishing jargon for "lines") are usually *either* horizontal or vertical in a table, but not both. (In
some types of printing, costs soar if tabular rules
must intersect.)

In addition:

1) Tables, like footnotes, may be numbered consecutively chapter by chapter or throughout an entire
   book.
2) Footnotes to tables—as opposed to footnotes occurring in the regular text—are usually symbols (*,
   †, ‡, etc.) or lowercase superscript letters ([a, b,] etc.).
   Occasionally they may be superscript numbers,
   but these are usually not used because the table
   itself frequently consists of numbers. These footnotes occur at the bottom of the table, *not* at the
   bottom of the text page.

3) Footnotes to tables can be consecutive going across the table or reading down each column of the table. The method depends on how the table is to be read. For example, a table listing each individual state, its population, and its area on a single line would have footnotes reading across the table:

Alabama	3,444,165[a]	51,609
Alaska[b]	302,173	586,412[c]

If the individual state was listed at the head of each vertical column with information pertinent to the state listed below, then footnotes would be consecutive down the column, not across.

4) Be certain the table is referred to in the text ("see Table 1"). Note that the reference should not say "see Table 1 below," for in type Table 1 may be "below" or it may be on the next page.

Lists

Numbering and punctuation should be consistent in lists. The author may refer to items (1), (2), and (3), or items (a), (b), and (c). Or she may use Roman numerals or capital letters. She may use full parentheses (one at the beginning and one at the end) or just a final parenthesis. Or she may omit parens and put a period after the number or letter. Or she may use parens and a period. Whatever she chooses, it should be consistent.

Lists may be run in with the text (an integral part of the text). In that case the copy editor has to make certain only that lists are identified consistently throughout the book (numbers or letters followed by periods or no periods, parens or no parens). However, lists standing separately from the text have to be perused more carefully. The first line of such lists may be flush left (aligning with the left-hand border of the text) *or* paragraph indented. Lines after the first line may be either flush left or indented to fall under the first word of text (called "hanging indent"). Thus

1.) This is one way
it could be set.

(a) This is another
way to do it.

Punctuation of lists not run in with the text should also be consistent throughout the book. If each entry is not a full sentence, the author may use a comma or semicolon after each one and a final period. Or he may omit all such punctuation (a more modern style).

In addition:

1) If a list is numbered past nine, the compositor should be instructed in a margin note to "clear for 10." This means to set the first nine one-digit numbers so that they will align with the two-digit numbers. (Lists in this book are "cleared for 10"; see pages 3–4 for an example.)

2) Lists set in two (or more) side-by-side columns may read across the page or down each column. It is usually better to have them read across the page; a downward-reading list may fall on two separate pages, forcing the reader to go back and forth. (For an example of this, see page 62.)

Extracts

Quotes from other sources may be run in with the text and identified by quotation marks; or they may be centered on the page. A frequently used rule of thumb is to center quotes of over five lines. Here is an example:

In his memoirs the general recalled: "There I was, alone, deserted by my men. Suddenly a beautiful apparition appeared from behind a nearby boulder. 'Have faith in God and country,' she urged. I meditated for a moment, then retrieved my rifle and went to meet the enemy."

In his memoirs the general recalled:

> There I was, alone, deserted by my men. Suddenly a beautiful apparition appeared from behind a nearby boulder. "Have faith in God and country," she urged. I meditated for a moment, then retrieved my rifle and went to meet the enemy.

Note that centering the quote serves to identify it, so quotation marks are not used.

In addition:

1) Most publishers do *not* want the style of an extract changed to conform with the general style of the manuscript. Thus a manuscript may use the spelling *ax*, but *axe* should be retained in the extract if it was used in the original quotation.

2) Many publishers require permission from the copyright holder for quotations of 100 words or more from a single copyrighted source (some publishers want permission for all quotes; some have different word limits). Permission is also needed for quoting even one line of a copyrighted poem or one line of music (words or notes). The copy editor may be asked to list such quotes and/or to check permissions already received.

Bibliography

Copy editors are frequently given instructions by the publisher as to the style for bibliographies. If not instructed, the copy editor should use the author's style (or select one of her styles if she mixes them). Some professional organizations are very picky as to the format they want used, so the copy editor—as usual—must not follow her own personal preference.

The copy editor is rarely expected to doublecheck bibliographical information. This can be done, however, by consulting *Books in Print* (published yearly by R. R. Bowker Co., New York), or the card catalog in libraries. As mentioned before, the copy editor should crosscheck bibliographical information against references that occur in the body of the manuscript. She must also make certain that all pertinent information is included in the bibliographical reference: author, title, publisher, place and year of publication.

Stylistically, a bibliography should be checked for consistency in:

1) Order of authors' names when there are two or more authors of a single book: Jones, John, and Eugene O'Neill *or* Jones, John, and O'Neill, Eugene.

2) Abbreviations used to identify editors ("Ed." or "ed." or "Editor" or "editor") and translators.

3) Identifying publishers: The full name can be written out (Dodd, Mead & Company) or a short form can be used (Dodd, Mead; Macmillan; etc.). The short form is more common.

4) Other frequently used words: Vol. *or* vol.; page *or* p. (pages *or* pp.); chapter *or* chap.; etc.

5) Identifying place of publication: The city and state can be given ("Newark, N.J."), or the state can be omitted if the city is well known. Thus "New York" (for New York, N.Y.) but "Englewood Cliffs, N.J."

6) Correct alphabetical order.

COPYEDITING SYMBOLS

Standard symbols have been devised for copyediting, so that editors, compositors, proofreaders, and authors will know precisely what changes are to be made. These symbols become automatic after you use them for a while.

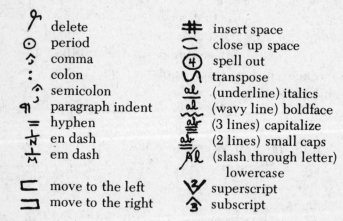

℘	delete	#	insert space
⊙	period	( )	close up space
⌃	comma	ⓢⓟ	spell out
⫶	colon	∽	transpose
⌃	semicolon	al al	(underline) italics
¶	paragraph indent	al al	(wavy line) boldface
=	hyphen	al al	(3 lines) capitalize
⊣N⊢	en dash	al al	(2 lines) small caps
⊣M⊢	em dash	Al	(slash through letter) lowercase
⊏	move to the left	v3	superscript
⊐	move to the right	ʌ3	subscript

Corrections are made *directly in the body of the manuscript*. They are *not* made in the margin. Obviously a manuscript must be typed double-spaced in order to provide enough room to make changes.

There is a very logical reason for marking in the body of the manuscript: The compositor works with the manuscript pages just as a typist works with copy.

He clips the pages up at his side as he sits at a keyboard. He reads the manuscript word for word—letter for letter, in theory—just as a typist does. If changes are marked in the margin, he constantly has to shift his eyes away from the word he is currently reading, losing his place for a second and cutting down on his speed (and his time is expensive!).

Similarly, it is very time consuming—costly—to ask a compositor to pick up a paragraph from one manuscript page and insert it on another page. He has to stop what he is doing, shuffle pages, find the insert. Or two compositors may be working concurrently on one manuscript. Compositor A will then have to trudge over to Compositor B to get the page with the insert. More money down the drain.

Suppose a copy editor wants to transfer a paragraph from page 64 to page 48. (She could just query the change, but let's assume the author or editor has marked the change, or it is so obvious and vital that the copy editor is just going to make it.) Most publishers prefer a complete cut-and-paste job: Cut the paragraph from page 64 and cut page 48 at the point where the paragraph is to be inserted. Then, on a new sheet of typing paper, paste or tape the text from page 48 followed by the paragraph from page 64 followed by the remaining text from page 48. This may require two pieces of paper; the page should not run longer than regular 8½" x 11" typing paper. What remains of page 64 will also have to be pasted or taped to another piece of paper.

The copy editor may also completely retype page 48 to include the paragraph from page 64. (The typing must be carefully proofread.) Or, if the material to be transposed is short, it can be neatly printed in place on page 48. It can also be typed or neatly written on the *top* margin of the page, and an arrow drawn around it indicating where it is to be inserted. (Do not write an insert on the bottom margin or sideways on the paper.)

HYPHENS AND DASHES

In the preceding list of symbols, note the hyphen (-), en dash (–), and em dash (—).

red-haired girl (hyphen)
a score of 8–3 (en dash)
Let's go—after dinner (em dash)

The en dash is the width of the letter *n* in the particular type being used to set the book; the em dash is the width of an *m* in that type.

The hyphen, as a symbol, needs little explanation. When typed in a manuscript it usually requires no additional copyediting mark. The exception is a hyphen occurring at the end of a line of type:

She emigrated from an English⸗
speaking colony.

She refused to marry the English-
man back home.

In the first example the hyphen is to be retained. This information is conveyed to the compositor by marking a double hyphen (it will look like an "equals" sign). If an end-of-line hyphen is not so marked, the compositor will automatically run the word together.

It is absolutely unnecessary to mark hyphens to be deleted at the end of a line. However, occasionally a copy editor will indicate that a hyphen is to be deleted so the proofreader will know it was not ignored through oversight. "Reelect" and similar words might be so marked.

This transaction is to be a non‑
negotiable bank loan.

The en dash is most frequently used in lieu of the word "to":

chapters 1–5   Genesis 1:3–8
1971–72   Detroit–Newark flight
May–June 1972   Queen Elizabeth (1926–   )

This symbol is typed as a hyphen, and the copy editor must always mark it for the compositor.

The en dash is also used in place of a hyphen in a compound adjective:

pre–Civil War South   German–Scotch-Irish heritage

An en dash may also be used in a heading in place of a hyphen if the publisher prefers:

CHAPTER I: ABLE–BODIED SEAMEN

In two specific instances an en dash may seem appropriate at first glance but is incorrect usage. First, never use an en dash if the word "from" is used:

She reigned from 1933 *to* 1972.
From May *to* December she abstained.

Second, never use an en dash if the word "and" can be substituted:

Between 6:30 *and* 6:40 she exercises.

An end-of-line en dash, like all en dashes, must be marked for the compositor.

The em dash is most often used to mark a sudden break in thought, a parenthetical aside, or an unfinished sentence.

Can you—will you—accept this gift?
You—you coward.
Her I.Q.—don't ask me mine—is 133.
"I love him, but—" she sighed.

All em dashes, including those at the end of a line, must be marked for the compositor.

There is also a 2-em dash (double the width of an *m*), which is usually used to indicate missing letters:

Miss S—— has been seen with Mr. H——.

And there is a 3-em dash (triple the width of an *m*), which is most commonly used in bibliographies to indicate the same author as the preceding entry:

Heinz, Tom, . . .
—— and John Campbell [Heinz and Campbell collaborated]

In addition to these standard copyediting symbols, it is sometimes necessary to write directions to the compositor directly on the manuscript, in the margin by the text. The note should be circled, indicating it is not an integral part of the text. The need for a note is most likely to occur in the following instances.

1) Underlining a word indicates it is to be set in italics. However, if the publisher wants the word to be actually underlined ("underscored" in publishing jargon . . . and often an expensive procedure), the compositor should be told: "Comp: underscore, do not set ital."

2) The # symbol indicates space is to be inserted. However, if the symbol itself, meaning "number," is wanted, a note should be written: "Comp: number symbol."

3) Slash marks, as in "and/or," can be confused for lines indicating space breaks. Therefore the copy editor should warn the compositor: "Comp: note slash mark." Brackets should also be identified, since they are not too clear when typed on a typewriter.

4) Symbols on foreign words—accent marks, cedillas, tildes, umlauts, Spanish upside-down question marks, the English symbol for pound (£), and other such symbols—should be called to the compositor's attention: "Comp: note cedilla [or whatever]." If this same symbol occurs time and again in a manuscript, most publishers only ask that a notation be made the first time: "Comp: note cedilla here and throughout." (Naturally the symbol itself must appear on the manuscript throughout.)

5) Mathematical symbols should be identified for the compositor. A subtraction sign looks like a hyphen, a multiplication sign looks like an x, a

division sign can look like a hyphen with some neatly spaced dots, an equals sign can look like a double hyphen: "Comp: note 'multiplication' sign [or whatever]."

6) Chapter titles and titles within a chapter—called heads—are usually set in type larger than the regular text and may be boldface, italics, small caps, or some other style. Rarely, the publisher gives the copy editor instructions for marking each head for the compositor. More frequently, the publisher codes the heads: A head, B head, etc. (infrequently, 1 head, 2 head). Coded heads need only be marked by inserting the proper code letter in the margin; they should *not* be marked for caps or italics or whatever might be wanted.

7) Similarly, text sometimes is coded. For instance, the publisher might want lists or centered quotes set in type that is smaller than the regular text type. A numerical code is usually given for this, and the copy editor merely has to bracket the material and write the code in a circle in the margin. In both heads and text, the code is usually devised by the publisher and explicit instructions are given to the copy editor.

8) A heavy black dot (●)—called a bullet—is often used to set off items in a list. It should be marked by the copy editor: "Comp: note bullet."

9) It is a good idea to ask the compositor to set black slugs (●●) where information is yet to come in a manuscript. For example: see page ●●. Or: 1945–194● (if the author is still hunting down this date). By calling for black slugs, which really

stand out, instead of just *O*'s or TK ("to come") or question marks, the copy editor is helping to ensure that the missing information will be filled in before the book reaches the public.

10) Finally . . . copy editors sometimes err. A word or sentence may be crossed out, and then the copy editor wants to put it back in. Rather than rewrite it, she can place dots under the crossed-out text. (Text should always be crossed out neatly, with a single line through it, and not scribbled and eradicated.) These dots tell the compositor to "stet" the deleted material ("stet" is a Latin imperative meaning "let it stand"). Thus

She is a ~~very~~ good girl

indicates that the word "very" is to be stetted— retained and set in type. These dots may also be used under very unusual spellings or other oddities in the manuscript, to indicate the copy editor noticed the word and wants it left as it appears:

Baseball stars Rogers Hornsby, Jimmy Foxx, Bo Belinsky

SAMPLE COPYEDITED PAGE

Here is a typed manuscript page, with all the corrections made by the copy editor. On the next page is the same material set in type. (You will find more examples of "correct" copyediting in the sample tests in Appendix IV.)

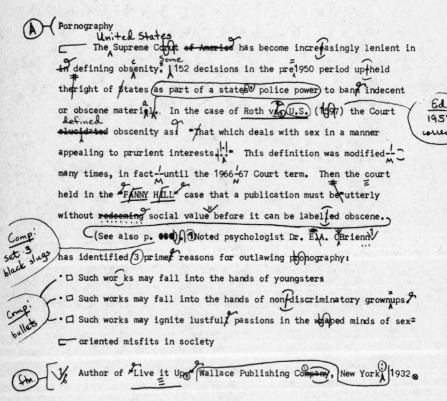

Pornography

The United States Supreme Court has become increasingly lenient in defining obscenity. Some 152 decisions in the pre-1950 period upheld the right of states to ban indecent or obscene material as part of a state's police power. In the case of *Roth v. United States* (1957) the Court defined obscenity as "that which deals with sex in a manner appealing to prurient interests. . . ." This definition was modified—many times, in fact—until the 1966–67 Court term. Then the Court held in the *Fanny Hill* case that a publication must be "utterly without redeeming social value" before it can be labeled obscene. (See also p. •••.)

Noted psychologist Dr. E. A. O'Brienn [1] has identified three prime reasons for outlawing pornography:

· Such works may fall into the hands of youngsters
· Such works may fall into the hands of nondiscriminating grown-ups
· Such works may ignite lustful passions in the warped minds of sex-oriented misfits in society

[1]Author of *Live It Up*. New York: Wallace Publishing Co., 1932.

KINDS OF MANUSCRIPTS

A copy editor usually works with a manuscript fresh from the author's typewriter and the editor's pencil. This kind of manuscript is copyedited in the manner described in this chapter. Occasionally a copy editor will be called upon to work on copy that already has been in print—stories or articles compiled into an anthology, an American version of a book published abroad, a reissue of an out-of-print book. In handling this type of manuscript, the copy editor is usually told to go along with the existing style; frequently she is told to make *no* changes except to correct typographical errors. This becomes a matter of reading the manuscript and compiling a style sheet (is "grey" or "theatre" a typographical error or the style?). It is a matter of publisher's preference whether stories or articles compiled in one book will be copyedited as a whole or individually. Some publishers prefer that each separate author retain his distinctive style; many believe this chops up a book and reduces the attentiveness of readers.

In dealing with a work of fiction, the copy editor should keep a detailed style sheet of characters and locations. Say Gretchen is introduced on page 24 as a sweet young girl with braces on her teeth and long blond braids. She leaves the action for a while, and when she returns she still has braces but she "curses like a sailor and vehemently shakes her curly black bob." The copy editor should check ages, physical characteristics, traits, mannerisms, and any other identifying information in a work of fiction.

Similarly, locations must be checked; Tenafly, N.J., should not suddenly become Tenefly, N.Y. Discrepancies should be queried. Since copy editors cannot possibly remember information for every character and locale, it is best to keep a style sheet pinpointing these details. This should be separate from the regular style sheet for the book. It usually is just for the copy editor's use and is not turned in with the finished manuscript and regular style sheet.

REMUNERATION

A 1973 survey of publishers who used freelance copy editors indicated the range of pay was from $3 to

$6 per hour. (Many publishers revealed only that their rates "vary.") Based on information from publishers who gave exact amounts, the average hourly rate for freelance copy editors was $5.[10]

From seven to ten pages an hour is the normal copyediting pace for an average, not-too-technical, not-too-simplistic manuscript. (What manuscript is average?) If considerable rewriting or research is involved, the number of pages per hour decreases accordingly. Experienced copy editors may do more than ten pages an hour; however, as discussed in Chapter 2, they usually charge seven to ten pages an hour in order not to be penalized for speedy work based on years of training and practice. Copy editors asked to do extensive retyping of a sloppy manuscript should charge their hourly copyediting rate for this extra service.

SUPPLIES AND BOOKS

Supplies

Red pencils with erasers (on rare occasions a publisher will ask a copy editor to use another color if red writing is already on the manuscript. A blue pencil should be avoided if possible, for publishers often Xerox copyedited manuscripts as a precaution against loss, and blue pencils frequently do not Xerox). If you do not write too heavily, a mechanical pencil with red lead is practical because it stays sharp.

Pencil sharpener.

[10]Since the publication of the first edition in 1974, freelance rates have gone up: In 1978, the range was, roughly, $4 to $7 per hour, with an average hourly rate of $6.

Tape (Scotch Magic Transparent Tape or Tuck Write-On Tape is best because it can be easily written on and erased).

Query tags (also called fliers), about 4¼" x 2¼", gummed along one short edge. These are attached to the edge of the manuscript at the point of the query—much better than writing on the manuscript page itself. Tags are sometimes given by publishers with manuscripts; they can also be obtained at some stationery stores. Use colored, not white tags—the white ones blend too easily with the manuscript page and might be overlooked.

Typewriter for retyping parts of a manuscript and preparing letters, resumes, and bills.

Typewriter paper, not the erasable kind. The manuscript must be handled by several people (author, editor, copy editor, production staff, compositor) and erasable paper smudges to illegibility and also slides out of order.

Inexpensive copier. This is certainly not necessary, but it is very handy for copying manuscript pages if you want to rewrite or reorganize but do not have carte blanche permission and must merely suggest changes; or for copying sections of a reference book for your own use. It is also valuable for out-of-town copy editors, who can promise to keep a copy of the copyedited manuscript in case the original is lost in the mails.

BOOKS

The following books are listed in Appendix II with all pertinent publishing information.

Along with the indispensable Webster's dictionary

(the desk dictionary will suffice, although it is ideal to have the Third Unabridged also) and *Words into Type* and *A Manual of Style,* other particularly useful books for copy editors include:

Good English grammar text (Strunk and White's *The Elements of Style* is superb; Fowler's *Modern English Usage* is a classic).

A "how-to" book on the intricacies of copyediting and freelancing (such as the one you are reading right now!).

Thesaurus.

Atlas or gazetteer.

Current almanac.

Dictionary other than Webster's (an unabridged dictionary or an encyclopedic one such as *The Reader's Digest Great Encyclopedic Dictionary* is extremely useful because of the additional words and terms listed there. In addition, most unabridged dictionaries have foreign-language, grammar, and atlas sections).

Specialized dictionaries (foreign language, scientific terms, cookery terms, and so on, depending on the kinds of manuscripts you copyedit).

Specialized source books (*The MLA Style Sheet* if you do many scholarly books; books of quotations; and so on).

Encyclopedia, for running down facts and dates.

Also, to keep up-to-date on current news as well as changing language styles, a copy editor must regularly read a nationally recognized newspaper. A good news magazine is also helpful. The trade publication *Publishers Weekly* will keep you abreast of news in the world of publishing.

Chapter 4

PROOFREADING: LIKE WATCHING A TENNIS VOLLEY

To someone who has never tried it, proofreading may seem to be the easiest job in editorial freelancing. In theory it is indeed a snap: The proofreader looks at words that have been set in type and reproduced on proofs, and makes certain they correspond exactly to those in the manuscript at hand. Back and forth she reads, from proofs to original copy, as if watching a tennis volley. If "supercalifragilistic" is on the manuscript, "supracalifragilistic" should not be set in type. If this mistake occurs, the proofreader marks the required change. If a transposition such as "famliy" appears, the proofreader merely corrects it. Of course, catching even such simple mistakes as these is not always as easy as it seems. An active brain tend to automaticaly fill in or or correct missing or tranposed letters; an inactive brain usaully will not recognize the prolbem at all. (Seven errors in the preceding sentence.)

This natural tendency of a functioning mind is one reason proofreading is much more difficult than it would appear. In order to catch typographical errors, the proofreader must read letter for letter . . . and even first-graders are taught never to read this way, for it is very time-consuming and does not facilitate reading comprehension. As children we learn that little squiggles are letters, and combinations of letters are words with some generally understood meaning. We come to recognize familiar words and phrases immediately, and do not really pick out individual letters—a decided drawback in proofreading. To compensate for this, a very successful managing editor of *The New York Times* latched onto the idea of proofreading by reading upside down. A similar method is to read each paragraph from *end to beginning;* involved is meaning no since reading word-for-word requires this.

If the proofreader was responsible only for making certain the compositor had faithfully set in type all the letters and spaces on a manuscript, the backward-reading method would be quite effective. But this is only one aspect of the work. In addition, the proofreader must check to see that the compositor has done those tasks directly delegated to him, such as following specific instructions of the editor or copy editor, dividing words correctly at the end of a line, spacing properly between words and between lines, accurately aligning the type, and using the correct kind of type.

And the proofreader has one more responsibility: making certain there are no errors on the original manuscript. Errors may be due to careless copyediting ("goodby" on page 12 of the manuscript, "goodbye" on page 48; "sieze" on page 73; "Katherine of

Aragon" on page 92). Or there may be factual mistakes that the proofreader can catch because of her general knowledge.

Thus the "simple" job of proofreading, often pooh-poohed in publishing circles, is truly a difficult one requiring real concentration. In a single reading the proofreader must do a myriad of things—and come as close to perfection as humanly possible. And she must initial everything she reads, accepting responsibility. In the chain of publishing, words omitted or misspelled by the manuscript typist should be picked up by the author; author errors should be corrected by the editor; editor oversights should be caught by the copy editor. But the proofreader is the end of the line; thousands of readers will be her judge.

PROFILE OF A SUCCESSFUL PROOFREADER

Basically, a proofreader must discipline herself to read painstakingly; can spot misspelled words; has an understanding of style; and is able to accept decisions that have been made by the author, editor, or copy editor.

The ability to read slowly and methodically is the prime attribute of a good proofreader. Even a slow reader must train herself to look at each individual letter, punctuation mark, and space, while still grasping the meaning of what is being read. Someone who has taken a course in speed reading will have a particularly difficult time becoming a successful proofreader, for everything learned in such a course must be blotted from the mind. Numbers and foreign words that are not understood are easiest to proofread in this slow manner, for they obviously must be checked against the original manuscript.

Read the following sentence slowly.

FROZEN FOODS ARE THE RESULT OF YEARS OF SCIENTIFIC STUDY AND THE DEVELOPMENT OF REFRIGERATION.

Now count aloud the *f*'s in that sentence. Count only once.

The average person finds four *f*'s. Identifying all seven is unusual—an indication of a mind already attuned to letter-by-letter reading. Because the mind knows there is an *f* in the unimportant word "of," it is difficult to recognize the letter when reading for sense as well as for *f*'s. This is the proofreader's dilemma: She must read slowly enough to let her mind become cognizant of every detail caught by the eye, but not so slowly that the grouped letters do not convey meaning.

In proofreading a mystery novel or other fascinating book, it is sometimes best to first read through for pleasure. Then the proofreader can get down to the real task ahead.

The ability to spot misspellings is the second important attribute of a successful proofreader. When asked to spell a tricky word aloud, many people will come up with the right combination of letters. They "know" how to spell it. But give them a typed sentence with a misspelled word. Many people will now have difficulty deciding if the tricky word is spelled correctly.

Words set in type tend to look right at first glance. Incorrectly spelled more than twice, they invariably look right. There is probably a mysterious psychological reason for this, perhaps traceable to our early learning from books and a sense of "sacredness" about the printed word. That something set in type is probably correct is a widely held notion—except by people who have worked in the publishing industry for a while. Proofreaders, the last professionals to carefully review a book before it reaches the public, must be especially alert for misspellings.

Once a person passes a rather tender age it takes real effort to learn spellings. Many of the words in well-researched lists of spellings that are bugaboos for high-schoolers turn up again in lists for collegians and business professionals; the professionals still cannot spell words that were troublesome during high school years.

Being human, proofreaders also have some spelling difficulties. The trick is to identify such words, then either learn them, look them up every time they appear, or create some mnemonic device for remembering them. For example, one of the authors of this book gets hopelessly vexed with "siege," "seize," and "weird." To remember, she repeats: Break the siege/and seize the weirdo. Similarly: A *pie*ce of pie. Station*e*ry is for l*ette*rs. (Don't rely on "Station*a*ry is p*a*per"!) Such extreme measures are sometimes necessary when a person is too lazy to memorize or has a mental block preventing her from learning. Also, trying to commit to memory a mnemonic device ofttimes leads to learning the correct spelling.

Proofread the following extremely tricky words. List—and spell correctly—those that you think are wrong. Do not refer to a dictionary. (Answers follow.)

abcess	accommodate	acknowlege
anoint	apparatus	asprin
assinine	bagle	batallion
Carribean	category	cellophane
cemetery	Cincinnati	collosal
commitment	compatent	consensus
consistancy	cooly	definitely
desparate	deterrent	develope
dietitian	diptheria	discernible
dissipate	dociley	drunkeness
ecstasy	ecxema	embarrass
exhilarate	friccasee	fullfill
gaiety	geneology	giggolo
grievence	harass	hemorrhage
hiefer	hypocracy	immaculate
inadvertent	incalcuble	incidently
independent	indispensible	inflammation
inoculate	iridescent	irresistable
jackal	jewelery	knickknack
liasion	mackarel	maintenance
mathmatics	mischevous	missile
misspelling	niece	occasion
occured	parallel	paraphernalia
perenially	permissable	pharoh
Philippines	Pittsburg (Pa.)	plebian
Portugese	prarie	preceed
predictible	preferred	propeller
recommend	religous	repetition
sacrilegious	seceed	seive
seize	separate	siege
spoonfull	supercede	syphillis
tassel	threshold	Tuscon
vengeance	vicious	wierd

The following words were misspelled in the preceding list but are correct here. Count as a mistake any word that you thought was misspelled but did not spell correctly. Fewer than 5 wrong, you are a genius speller (and pretty lucky!); from 5 to 10 wrong, you are mighty good; 10 to 15 wrong, you are average; more than 15 wrong, you had better refer to a dictionary frequently.

abscess	acknowledge	aspirin
asinine	bagel	battalion
Caribbean	colossal	competent
consistency	coolly	desperate
develop	diphtheria	docilely
drunkenness	eczema	fricassee
fulfill	genealogy	gigolo
grievance	heifer	hypocrisy
incalculable	incidentally	indispensable
irresistible	jewelry	liaison
mackerel	mathematics	mischievous
occurred	perennially	permissible
pharaoh	Pittsburgh (Pa.)	plebeian
Portuguese	prairie	precede
predictable	religious	secede
sieve	spoonful	supersede
syphilis	Tucson	weird

Besides knowing basic spelling, the proofreader must know which alternative spellings have been selected for the manuscript at hand. Choosing an alternative is the job of the author/editor/copy editor, and the proofreader should have a style sheet prepared by the copy editor. Alternatives include such words as adviser/advisor; catsup/ketchup; guerrilla/guerilla; OK/okay; resume/résumé; lit/lighted; clueing/cluing; ghettos/ghettoes. Alternative endings include labeled/labelled; worshiper/worshipper.

The final attribute of a successful proofreader is that she be rather humble and willing to go along with decisions already made. A proofreader has no decisionmaking powers, no inherent right to reword or rearrange or restyle a manuscript *unless specifically instructed to do so by the publisher*. A proofreader may suggest changes if she believes they are really vital. She should correct faulty grammar or misspellings. But basically she must accept the manuscript as it has been presented to the compositor. This specific lack of responsibility is what gives proofreading its reputation as a cinch job. Sometimes it is very difficult for a proofreader to hold her peace; the desire to make decisions is probably the reason many proofreaders switch to copyediting.

BECOMING A PROOFREADER

Most people have had some proofreading experience: checking the final typed version of a term paper, catching errors while reading a book, actual experience on a high school or college newspaper. The experience of typing copyedited manuscripts is also helpful for a proofreader, for it teaches the meaning of basic symbols used to give directions for typesetting.

It is not too difficult to become a proofreader, for it is more a matter of knowing what to look for and being perceptive than of extensive training. Studying a chapter such as this one will set you on the right path. Then it becomes a matter of keeping the various points in mind and making sure you look for them. A concise list of major points appears on page 107. It may be helpful to have an experienced proofreader review your first efforts to see if you are overlooking significant aspects of proofreading, such as checking for proper end-of-line hyphenization or broken type.

In applying for a freelancing job, you should send a thorough resume (see Chapter 2). Some publishers require that applicants take a test, usually at home. The test will probably be a completely garbled typesetting job. It is not uncommon to have someone else also proofread the test after you have finished; there will be so many errors that you are very likely to miss several you would catch in normal copy. Appendix IV includes four sample proofreading tests to help you prepare yourself.

Some publishers have adopted a splendid idea of sending out a proofreading job to a new applicant, then carefully checking her work when it is returned. If there are only a few errors (every proofreader overlooks something occasionally), the applicant will be sent more work. This is a much fairer and more logical way of testing.

Freelance proofreaders usually get paid by the hour. A few publishers pay by the job, which is fine if you are relatively quick. On the average, a proofreader reads from four to six galleys per hour (naturally this depends on the size of the type, the width of the line, and the complexity of the material).

PROOFREADING GALLEYS

Normally a proofreader reads galleys, long sheets of cheap paper on which the type has been printed. There are no page breaks on galleys . . . the type just runs on and on. One galley usually equals two to three book pages. Most books that analyze proofreading seem to assume it will be done by two people, one reading the copy aloud and the other following along on the galley. This is ideal. But in the real world, proofreading is a one-person job.

The proofreader looks for three things when reading galleys: (1) faithful reproduction of the manuscript; (2) flaws in setting the type; (3) consistency and accuracy of the manuscript itself.

Faithful Reproduction

Transposed or omitted letters are hard enough to spot if just reading galleys as you would read a book. But checking for faithful reproduction necessitates reading against copy, comparing the words set in type with the original manuscript. A compositor may set a word that looks right even in context but is not what is on the manuscript. For example, "He is her blond relative" when the manuscript states "He is her blood relative." If not reading the galley against copy, the proofreader might well miss the small problem of *n* rather than *o*. The compositor may also completely forget to set a word or a line or even a whole paragraph. Only by comparing the galley with the copy can the proofreader pick up such typographical errors, called "typos" or "PE's" (printer's errors).

Proofreaders should be particularly alert in reading chapter titles and other large-size heads. It is very easy to miss typos set in big print. Even the staid *New York Times* occasionally comes up with some headlined whoppers:

CENTRAL SYNAGOGUE CELEBRATES IT'S BIGINNING 100 YEARS AGO

ATTENDS FUNERAL IN THE CAPITAL FOR JUSTICE BLACK NIXON

Books as well as journals are susceptible to careless proofreading of large type.

COMPOSITOR'S PERSONAL ERRORS

The compositor is directly responsible for some aspects of setting type, and the proofreader must verify that he has done his job properly. His main personal responsibility is word divisions at the end of a line. Say the word "thousand" must be hyphenated because it will not fit on one line; is "thou-sand" or "thous-and" correct? "Di-saster" or "dis-aster"? "Perfor-mance" or "perform-ance"? "Defin-ition" or "defini-tion"?

In making these decisions a compositor follows *Webster's Third International* or *Seventh New Collegiate Dictionary* (the standard dictionaries used in publishing). To make certain that words have been correctly hyphenated, the proofreader must look up in Webster's any questionable divisions. (Just as a point of interest, note that Americans divide words according to pronunciation; British divisions are based on derivation. Thus "democ-racy" in the U.S., "demo-cracy" in the U.K.)

Word division can become quite involved,[1] but the proofreader will be in fine shape if she follows the word divisions in Webster's and the following guide-lines:

1) One-letter word divisions are never acceptable: a-plomb, are-a, and such.
2) Two-letter word divisions are permissible at the *end* of a line of type, but many publishers do not allow them at the beginning of a line:

That proofreader is en-grossed in her work.

That proofreader seeks mon-ey, not perfection.

The division in the first sentence is perfectly all right. The second sentence should be pointed out on the galley in a note to the publisher—unless the proofreader has been given instructions about two-letter finales.

3) Large numbers may be divided after a comma, unless the publisher forbids this: $148,320,000,-000.
4) Symbols and abbreviations used with figures should not be hyphenated: $62.35, £5 4s., 72 ft., 3 lb., 12 B.C., 3:45 A.M., and the like must be set on a single line.
5) Abbreviations must not be divided. This includes initials used in place of a person's first and middle names. (*B.-O. Smith* is not acceptable. *B.O.-Smith* is allowable, although it is better to include the full name on one line if possible.) All other abbre-

[1] For a thorough examination of the nuances of word division, see *A Manual of Style:* The University of Chicago Press, Chicago, 1969, pp. 132, 137–39.

viations (U.S.S.R., UNICEF, and so on) should be set on a single line.

Similarly, many publishers do not want the final line of a paragraph to be merely the last part of a word. This is especially true if only a few letters occur on the last line. (Aesthetically this is undesirable, because the empty space after a short line breaks up the block of type on the page.) Such short end-of-paragraph lines should be noted on the galley for the publisher, who will decide whether to spend the money rectifying the problem. Also, short words (two, three, or four letters) on a line alone at the end of a paragraph are considered substandard form and should be noted on the galley (unless the proofreader is told to ignore them). These short lines are called "widows."

The proofreader must know copyediting symbols (see page 74) in order to determine if the compositor has faithfully reproduced the manuscript. These symbols are much the same as those used by proofreaders, although there are additional symbols that are used only in proofreading. (The use of proofreading symbols is discussed later in this chapter.)

Some copyediting symbols may be somewhat unclear to a new proofreader. One is a circle around a number or word, which means "spell it out." Thus "5" enclosed in a circle on the manuscript means to write out "five"; "U.S." in a circle means to write out "United States."

Another possible source of misunderstanding is a double hyphen at the end of a line. This indicates the hyphen is to be retained; a single hyphen at the end of a line indicates the word is to be run in.

Freelancers are good-͞	Freelancers are good-
natured folk.	ly people.

Set in type, these would read:

Freelancers . . . good-natured folk.
Freelancers . . . goodly people.

Another compositor responsibility that the proof-reader should be aware of is the kind of type used for punctuation marks. A mark should be set in the same type as the word, letter, or symbol immediately preceding. Thus if the final word is in italics, the following quotation mark, exclamation mark, comma, colon, or semicolon should be set in italics (there is no italic period). If the last word is in boldface, the punctuation mark (including a period) should be in boldface. Note that parentheses and brackets are almost always set in roman (regular) type, not in italics or boldface.

PREFERRED	NOT STANDARD
She is so *fast!*	She is so *fast*!
Is this section 2*a*?	Is this section 2*a*?
Note: set in boldface.	**Note**: set in boldface.

Occasionally the publisher will want some variation; for example, roman punctuation following a single italic or boldface letter (as in the second example). The publisher tells the compositor of any desired variation in standard practice, and the proofreader should also be informed. If such a variation crops up consistently on the galleys and the proofreader has not been told, she should query the publisher by list-

ing the galley numbers and lines where the variations occur. She should *not* mark the punctuation to
be changed, for it is likely the compositor knows
what he is doing (compositors tend to be extremely
alert) and the proofreader has just not been told.

Contrariwise, apostrophe-*s* endings of proper
nouns should be set in roman type when the word is
set in italics: *Redbook*'s readership (not *Redbook's*),
Titanic's voyage (not *Titanic's*). The proofreader
must check that this is done correctly.

The proofreader must also be alert for broken letters on the galley. It is often difficult to identify a
broken letter as opposed to a bad inking job that
makes the letter appear light. Basically, a broken letter has a flaw—perhaps a little hole or crack—and the
same letter with the same flaw will occur intermit-
tently in the galleys. If a certain letter seems to be
always broken, or a great many in a row seem broken, it is probably just poor inking. The compositor
has more than one type mold for every letter, and the
chance of every single piece being similarly flawed is
remote. Note the broken "g" in this example:

Tony hates dogs.

Similarly, some letters may have hairline marks sur-
rounding them (this occurs most frequently with
italics):

Dogs|love|Tony.

The proofreader should mark broken letters and hair-
lines by circling the imperfect letter, then placing an
x in a circle in the margin of the galley.

When the type is being arranged for printing, one or more lines may slip out of vertical alignment. Or an individual letter or word may be too high or too low. The proofreader should mark these to be aligned properly.

Finally, questions from the compositor or the compositor's proofreader may appear on galleys. These usually concern spelling, punctuation, grammar, or an omitted word. The publisher's proofreader should answer queries whenever possible. For example, a manuscript sentence may read, "She are pretty." The compositor will probably set this, then his proofreader may circle "are" on the galley and ask, "Ed: is?" The publisher's proofreader need only cross out the question mark at the end of the query, affirming that "is" is correct. If "are" was the correct word—for some far-out reason—the entire query should be crossed out, which tells the compositor to leave the type as set. Or, instead of setting "are" and querying it, the compositor might actually set "is." The note on the galley would then read, "Ed: OK?" If the publisher's proofreader agrees, she crosses out the question mark at the end of the query, affirming that the compositor's change was fine. If the change was not correct, the proofreader crosses out "is" and writes "are" in the margin; she also crosses out the query.

MANUSCRIPT CONSISTENCY AND ACCURACY

Besides being certain the compositor has faithfully reproduced the manuscript and has accurately performed his own tasks, the proofreader must check the manuscript for consistency and accuracy. The proofreader does this by referring to the style sheet that should accompany every manuscript. The copy editor compiles the style sheet, listing the alternatives chosen for punctuation, capitalization, abbreviations, spelling, numbers, special display matter (footnotes, tables, lists, extracts, bibliography). Examples of style are:

Jack, Jill, and pail/Jack, Jill and pail
May 1973/May, 1973
The Federal Government/the federal government
King John, the great king/King John, the great King
U.N. and N.A.T.O./UN and NATO/U.N. and NATO
traveling/travelling
Hernán Cortés/Hernando Cortez
the eleven competitors/the 11 competitors
pages (*or* pp.) 212–213/pages (*or* pp.) 212–13/pages (*or* pp.) 212–3
Jones, John, *Betsy Ross:* Baltimore, City Press, 1963./Jones, John. *Betsy Ross.* Baltimore: City Press, 1963. (And other styles)
Freelancers must be 1.) smart, 2.) diligent./Freelancers must be (a) smart, (b) diligent. (And other styles)

The proofreader assumes the manuscript is consistent, but uses the style sheet to doublecheck. (A proofreader with a photographic memory will be superb at this!) If the style sheet lists "kidnapping" but the manuscript consistently has "kidnaping," then something is amiss. Either there is a mistake on the style sheet, or the copy editor did not catch these words on the manuscript. In such a case the proofreader would list the galley number and line where each "kidnaping" occurred. The publisher would decide whether to add the extra p, as called for on the style sheet. A more frequent occurrence is a mixed style in the manuscript: half "kidnapping" and half "kidnaping." Then the proofreader would see what was on the style sheet and would change the galleys to correspond—either one *p* or two.

Comes the kicker: Few style sheets are complete. And all too often there is none at all. The proofreader must then add to the existing sheet or compile one from scratch. The choice of style alternatives should have been made before the manuscript was set in type, even if these choices were not listed. It is not the proofreader's job to make stylistic decisions (unless specifically asked to do so, which in effect is copyediting the galleys). However, the proofreader must check that the same alternative is used consistently. For this reason, proofreaders need to be aware of the elements of style; these are detailed on pages 47–74.

The proofreader will also have to use the style sheet to check any text being added to the galleys. It is her responsibility to make certain these additions conform to the style of the book.

The proofreader should also check that footnotes are in correct numerical order, alphabetization is right, chapter numbers follow one after the other, and chapter titles agree with the table of contents. Also, the editor or copy editor may have written queries to the author on the manuscript pages; if these are unanswered and have not been transferred to the galleys, the proofreader should write the queries beside the corresponding text on the galley. All page references in the body of the text will be blank, since pages have not been assigned; these should be brought to the publisher's attention by writing a note in the margin of the galley: "Ed: page number needed."

Changes should be marked directly on the galley whenever space permits. Changes will be (1) compositor's errors that must be corrected, (2) proofreader's corrections, (3) editor's or author's corrections or revisions. If a long change is being made, perhaps a few new sentences, it should be neatly written or typed on the bottom or top of the galley and a line drawn to indicate where it should be inserted. If there is not enough space to do this, the insert should be typed on a piece of paper, and the paper trimmed right around the typing so it is as small as possible. The slip should be pasted or taped to the margin of the galley near where it is to be inserted; the typed side should be *face up* on the galley. One or more full pages of inserts are attached in the same way: pasted or taped on top of the galley, print side up, near where the insertion is to be made. (It is important to remember that all inserts must be copyedited by the proofreader.) A paper clip or pin can also be used for added security, but do not rely solely on this, for the insert can easily become detached. Each insert should be marked "Insert for galley whatever-the-number-is." In the margin of the galley next to the spot where the insert is to be made, make a note: "see insert attached," with a caret showing exactly where the new material is to go. More than one typed addition per galley should be labeled "Insert A for galley 25," "Insert B for galley 25," etc.

Finally, the proofreader will score a big plus for any errors she finds in the manuscript. Authors, editors, and copy editors may not admit it, but they are human and can have blind spots. If the proofreader discerns an error in spelling or grammar, she should simply correct it on the galley if positive she is correct; if uncertain whether it is a matter of style, she should query the publisher by writing a note on the galley (there should not be many such queries). On the other hand, a possible factual error should always be queried on the galley, *not* corrected; the odds are 3 to 1 that it is not an error . . . author, editor, copy editor versus proofreader.

In essence, then, when reading galleys a proofreader is ever alert for the following:
1) The same letters and spaces as on the manuscript; no omissions, no additions, no transpositions.
2) Carrying out of all editor's and copy editor's instructions.
3) End-of-line hyphenization.
4) Type used for final punctuation.
5) Broken letters.
6) Hairline marks.
7) Vertical alignment of lines of type.
8) Horizontal alignment of letters.
9) Stylistic consistency.
10) Errors of spelling, grammar, or fact.

From this list it is clear why a galley with absolutely no marks except the proofreader's initials would be a real rarity.

PROOFREADING PAGE PROOFS

Galleys are also reviewed by the author and editor. Then the publisher will indicate page breaks on the galleys, taking into account illustrations; footnotes; and any tables, charts, or subheads that may have been grouped on separate galleys.

The proofread galleys, called the master proof or master set, are returned to the compositor, who makes all the text changes that have been indicated. Then a makeup man arranges the type into the separate pages that will be in the book. The pages are first printed on long sheets of cheap paper, like the galleys; these are called page proofs.

Page proofs are returned to the publisher to be checked against the master set of galleys (the original manuscript is now out of the picture). Usually the publisher's production department proofreads page proofs. Rarely are they freelanced—but rarely is not never. A few publishers do send out page proofs, so it is worthwhile for a proofreader to know the necessary procedures.

First and foremost: Page proofs are *not* read word for word like galleys. The proofreader merely reads the line on which the change was made and any subsequent lines that had to be reset because of the change. For example, say a word is inserted in line 4 of an eight-line paragraph. That one addition may necessitate changing not only line 4 but also lines 5, 6, 7, and 8. Thus the proofreader must read *all* the lines that have been reset, not just the obvious line where the change occurs.

Linotype is always produced in a full line, not letter by letter or word by word. Therefore when one letter is changed, the *entire line* is reset and must be proofread. Also, the line above the change and the line below it should be read. (When the makeup man pulls out a line of type and inserts a corrected line, it is possible that he will batter an adjoining line and have to reset it also. Or an adjoining line could slip out of position.) Monotype is set letter by letter, but the whole line—plus the line above and the line below—should be checked to make sure all letters are in their proper places.

Which leads to one of the most odious chores in proofreading: slugging pages. Each line of type is called a slug, and any single slug may become dislodged in the process of making up pages. Since a proofreader is not expected to read page proofs in their entirety, out-of-order lines could be easily overlooked. Therefore, after checking lines that have been reset, the proofreader compares galleys against pages—a process called slugging. This is done by folding each galley lengthwise to cover the first seven letters or so of each line of type. This folded galley is held against the page proofs, about seven letters in from the left-hand margin of the text.

The first seven letters on the page proof should run right into the letters on the galley. For example, "the pin-s" may appear on the page proof. The galley will be positioned so that "triped suit was gray . . ." continues the line. Thus by scanning the first eleven letters or so (seven letters on the page proof, four on the galley) the proofreader can make certain that all the lines on the galley are in the same order on the pages. The slugging will often be out of kilter where lines have been reset; these are the lines the proof-reader has read while checking corrections called for on the galleys.

Page numbers, called "folios," are inserted on page proofs. The proofreader must verify that these are consecutive. This is usually done all at one time, not in conjunction with other chores. (Note that page one and all subsequent odd-numbered pages always fall on the right-hand side of a book.)

On each page there is usually a "running head" (at the top) or a "running foot" (at the bottom). These are normally—but not necessarily—book title on the left, chapter title on the right. Each running head or foot must be proofread. (In page proofs, the *Reader's Digest Almanac* once had about eighty running heads "Untied States." An alert proofreader righted this wrong.) The proofreader should check the chapter title against the running head or foot.

The proofreader also checks to be sure there are no "widows." A few letters or a very short word at the end of any paragraph is called a widow, but is not particularly serious. Many publishers do not care at all about these (perhaps such short lines should be called divorcées?). The important widows are those that occur at the top of a page when the last line of a paragraph falls there. This line should not be shorter than the full width of the text, for a short line at the top of a solid block of text is deemed to be unat-tractive. The proofreader can bring such widows to the attention of the publisher by writing a note in the margin of the galley. Many publishers ask the proofreader to try to fill such lines rather than just note them. "Filling a line" means inserting a word or

two to make the line run all the way to the end of the
text block (but not to make a second line).

occurred in 1961 at a UN meeting.
  There is ample evidence that the conflict
would never have gotten out of hand if the

In this example, spelling out "United Nations"
would "kill" (get rid of) the widow. Or the proofreader might suggest adding "the year" before
"1961." The object is to add just enough letters to fill
the whole line. By counting the number of characters
and spaces in a full line of type, the proofreader can
approximate how many letters need to be added.
(The compositor can also add a little more space between words.) The proofreader indicates what should
be spelled out or added, then writes a marginal note
to the compositor: "Comp: set to full measure."
  Occasionally galleys are so marked up with
changes that revised galleys are obtained before page
proofs. These are proofread like page proofs, checking only changed lines plus the line above and the
line below, and slugging to be sure no lines are out
of order. Vice versa, every once in a while a manuscript is set directly into page proofs; the proofreader
must read these as she would read galleys.

PROOFREADING SYMBOLS

  The proofreader identifies changes that must be
made and brings them to the attention of the compositor, who will reset the lines. She calls attention to
changes by writing symbols in the *margin* of the gal-

ley or page proof. When the compositor scans the
margin he is immediately able to see which lines are
to be reset. If changes were made only in the body of
the text, with symbols squeezed between lines of
type, the compositor would have to read the entire
book to be certain of finding all the little marks.[2]

The following standard symbols are used by proofreaders. Note that proofreading is always a two-step
process: a mark is made in the body of the text and
also in the margin.

SYMBOL IN MARGIN	TEXT MARKINGS	MEANING
	How are you?	delete
	How are you?	close up
	How are you?	delete and close up
	How are you?	space
	How are you?	delete and space
	He is in the inn.	equal space
	Look alive, lady.	close up a little
	I'm fine And you?	period
	I'm fine thanks.	comma
	Note Go to jail.	colon
	He's thin she's fat.	semicolon
	Are you sure	question mark [3]
	I sure am	exclamation mark
	Hi," he said.	open quotation marks

[2] In contrast, a copy editor marks *only* in the body of the text, since the
compositor must read every word while setting the type.

[3] The word *set* should appear in the margin beside the question mark to
make sure the compositor sets the symbol: He might think the proofreader was merely questioning something. (If the proofreader did want to
question something, she should put a question mark in the margin and
enclose it in a circle. Anything circled is not to be set.)

SYMBOL IN MARGIN	TEXT MARKINGS	MEANING
᭡	"Hi, she replied.	close quotation marks
᭡	She̦s getting fat.	apostrophe
=	He's goodnatured.	hyphen
⊥	The Mets won 19/1.	en dash [4]
⊥ᴹ	Don't go yet.	em dash [4]
᭡²	$a^2 + b^2 = c^2$	superscript
᭡₂	H₂O	subscript
¶	"Let's go." "No."	paragraph
no ¶	I think: She is right.	no paragraph
tr.	She's deifting.	transpose
w.o.	Bread & butter	write out
~	Where is homa?	invert
≡	The united States	capitalize [5]
s.c.	In 409 b.c.	small caps
l.c.	The UNITED States	lowercase [6]
ital.	She reads the Times.	italics
rom.	The news was good.	roman [7]
bf	Is this boldface?	boldface
lf	Is this lightface?	lightface
wf	Robert or Richard	wrong font
X	Dogs	broken letter
⊓	She is here.	move up
⊔	She was there.	move down
⊏	Whaddya know?	move left
⊐	Don't know much.	move right

[4] The use of en and em dashes is explained on pp. 77–78.

[5] An alternate method used by many proofreaders is to put three lines under the letter to be capitalized and just write "cap" in the margin.

[6] The method as shown is preferable for lowercasing a number of successive letters. A line through each letter would be messy and hard to read.

[7] Roman type can best be defined negatively: It is *not* italic.

SYMBOL IN MARGIN	TEXT MARKINGS	MEANING
⊐⊏	The newspaper headline ⊐Strike Averted⊏ was welcome news to me.	center
(align)‖	‖The strike was arbitra- ted by union leaders as well as management.	align
(align)	The s_{tri}k_e ^wa_s eⁿd_{ed.}	align

Changes made by proofreaders fall into two categories: (1) inserting something new that the compositor has omitted or the author/editor now wants to add, and (2) deleting or changing something that has already been set in type. When something is to be inserted, the proofreader places a caret at the proper place in the text, then writes the insert in the margin.

M̲o̲/ George ∧Cohan was fabulous.

When something is to be deleted, the proofreader draws a line through it—being careful not to obliterate the text, for the compositor must be able to read what is to be deleted—and then makes a delete sign in the margin.

℺/   George M. Cohan was℺ fabulous.

Novice proofreaders are sometimes perplexed by the "delete," "delete and close up," and "delete plus space" symbols.

℺/ | Shee℺ is industrious. | (delete)
℺/ | Shĺe is industrious. | (delete and close up)
℺ #/ | Shee℺is industrious. | (delete plus space)

In the first example the proofreader merely wants the extra *e* deleted. In the second example the *h* must come out and the letters run together to make the word "she." In the last example the *e* has to be removed and space inserted between the two words.

Another possible problem is deleting one thing and inserting something in its place.

Cohan was a fabulous shoeman.   w/
Cohan is a fabulous showman.   was/
Cohan is a a fabulous shoeman.   ℈/w

A delete mark in the margin is not needed to remove the *e* or the word "is"; the marginal note brings the change to the compositor's attention while giving him additional instructions. In the third example, however, a marginal symbol is needed to delete "a" since the other change occurs elsewhere in the line.

One other point: When inserting a letter at the beginning or end of a word, a connecting mark should be used. This tells the compositor whether the letter goes at the end of one word or the beginning of the next.

d/   Here's the ice rink.
              ʌ

The marginal instruction on this outlandish example is not clear. A connection mark is needed to show where the *d* belongs.

⊃d/   Here's the ice rink.   (iced rink)
d⊃/   Here's the ice rink.   (ice drink)
              ʌ

All such insertions between words should be marked for connection in order to save the compositor's time and to ensure accuracy.

Here is a brief example of proofreading.

Proofreading changes are always indicated in the margin as well as in the body of the text. The compositor scans the margin and resets those lines that are marked. If changes were snuck into the line and not brought to the compositor's attention he would never find them.

This example would be reset by the compositor to read:

> Proofreading changes are always indicated in the margin as well as in the body of the text.
> The compositor scans the margin and resets those lines that are marked. If changes were snuck into the line and not brought to the compositor's attention he would never find them.

Marginal notes are arranged from left to right in the same order as the changes in the text. Slash marks separate changes when more than one is to be made in a single line of type. Usually all changes in one line are made either to the right of the text *or* to the left, depending on space available. (It is perfectly acceptable to put symbols for one line on the left, symbols for the next line on the right; readability is the criterion.) If there are oodles of changes on a specific line and they just will not fit on one side, they can start on the left and continue on the right. (This would be extremely unusual. If there were so many changes, it would be better to delete the entire line, then type or rewrite it on the top or bottom of the galley and mark it to be inserted.)

Occasionally the same change is wanted twice in a line. This is indicated in the margin by simply making two slash marks (providing there is no change in between).

The compositer is a very smart persen.
He is thin/ she is fat/ the dog is just right.
He is very thin, she is very fat.
He is very thin/ she is very fat.

Once in a while proofreaders change something on galleys and then decide they want to leave it the way it was. To tell the compositor that the original typesetting was correct, dots are placed under the crossed-out letter or word, and "stet" is written in the margin. "Stet" is Latin for "let it stand."

George O. Cohan was a fabulous shoeman.   STET

Here is an example of a proofread galley. This was read against the copyedited manuscript on page 82.

PORNOGRAPHY

The United States Supreme Court has become increasingly lenient in defining obscenity. Some 152 decisions in the pre1950 period upheld the right of states to ban indecent or obscene material as part of a states police power. In the case of *Roth v. United States* (1957), the Court defined obscenity as that which deals with sex in

a manner   appealing to prurient interests." This definition was ~~was~~ modified,
many times, in fact—until the 1966/67 court
term. Then the court held in the Fanny Hill
case that a publication must be "utterly without redeeming social value" before it can be
labelled obscene. (See also p. ●●●.)

Noted psychologist DR. E.A. O'Brienn has
identified three prime reasons for outlawing
pornography/
· Such works may fall into the hands ~~fall into the hands~~ of youngsters
· Such words may fall into the hands of non-
discriminatory grownups
Such works may ignite lustful passions in
the ~~warped~~ minds of sex-oriented ~~fismits~~ misfits in
society

¹ Author of *Live It Up*. New ~~Yrko:~~ Wallace Publishing
~~Company,~~ 1932.

The page proof (or corrected galley) would read
like this:

PORNOGRAPHY

The United States Supreme Court has become increasingly lenient in defining obscenity. Some 152 decisions in the pre-1950
period upheld the right of states to ban indecent or obscene material as part of a state's
police power. In the case of *Roth v. United
States* (1957), the Court defined obscenity as
"that which deals with sex in a manner appealing to prurient interests. . . ." This definition was modified—many times, in fact—
until the 1966–67 Court term. Then the Court
held in the *Fanny Hill* case that a publication
must be "utterly without redeeming social

PROOFREADING

119

value" before it can be labeled obscene. (See also p. ●●●.)

Noted psychologist Dr. E. A. O'Brienn [1] has identified three prime reasons for outlawing pornography:

· Such works may fall into the hands of youngsters
· Such works may fall into the hands of non-discriminatory grown-ups
· Such works may ignite lustful passions in the warped minds of sex-oriented misfits in society

[1] Author of *Live It Up.* New York: Wallace Publishing Co., 1932.

All errors made by the compositor should be marked PE (printer's error). PE should appear in a circle in the margin next to the symbol indicating what change is to be made. In the preceding example, all changes would be marked as PE's (the compositor would have ample reason to commit harakiri). An error that is not a PE is an AA (author's alteration . . . not "error," of course!). Most publishers only want the proofreader to put PE in the margin—all other changes are obviously AA's. It is vital to mark PE's because the compositor assumes the cost of resetting those lines; the publisher must pay for all other changes. (It can cost more than $5 to reset a single line of type.)

TYPOGRAPHY

Typography is basically a matter of setting letters and spaces so that they form the words called for on a manuscript. The size of the letters can vary from huge to minute; spaces in a line of type can also vary considerably.

Hobgoblinsandblackcats.
Hobgoblins and black cats.
Hobgoblins and black cats.
Hobgoblins and black cats.

The first example is set tight—no space between words. (This is frequently done with abbreviations, as in "Arkansas A&M" rather than "Arkansas A & M" or "U.S." rather than "U. S.") The second and third examples are both normal spacing. The fourth example is letterspaced (thin spaces between letters to widen the line).

Successive lines usually do not have exactly the same amount of space between words (note the lines on this page). This is because most books are "justified"—that is, set with perfectly aligned margins—and the width of letters varies. A line that is not justified is set "ragged right." Poetry is often set this way.

How does all this apply to proofreading? First, there may be a note on the copy telling the compositor to set something ragged right or to letterspace or to set tight. The proofreader has to verify that this has been done properly. Second, through oversight a line may not be justified. The proofreader would then write a marginal note: "Comp: justify line."

Third, very occasionally a "river of white" will appear in type. (This is not a PE.) This occurs when spaces between words happen to fall in a distinct, completely obvious pattern on succeeding lines. The pattern may be either vertical, as in the following example, or may angle down and across.

Proofreading is a more technical job
than merely looking for misspellings
and similar errors that could easily
be seen by any literate person.

The proofreader may do one of two things: (1) bring the "river of white" to the publisher's attention by noting it in the margin of the galley, or (2) try to fix it, and then tell the publisher what she's done: "Ed: note addition to eliminate river of white." Usually the only way to overcome a "river of white" is to change a word or to insert or delete a word. In the preceding example the word "other" could be inserted after "and" in the third line.

Proofreading is a more technical job
than merely looking for misspellings
and other similar errors that could
easily be caught by any literate person.

Similarly, the same word may just happen to fall in the same place on successive lines. Or there may be continuous end-of-line hyphens.

This is a good time to
analyze what is going to
happen if you decide to
become a freelancer.

Mary may be con-
trary but she's cer-
tainly an outstand-
ing gardener.

If either the same word or an end-of-line hyphen occurs *more than twice* in a row, it should be noted on the galley for the publisher. Or the proofreader can fix it by inserting or deleting or changing a word, then noting the change for the publisher: "Ed: note change to eliminate successive words [hyphens]." In the first example "is going to" might be changed to "could," which would reposition the words in that line. In the second example the entire word "outstanding" would probably fit on the third line, eliminating one of the hyphens.

Occasionally the proofreader will call for letterspacing as the only solution for a particular line of type. This is most likely to be necessary on a top-of-page widow or a very short line (as alongside a photograph).

Richard   M.   Nixon
cheered the ball team.

There is too much space between words in the first line of this example, which is set to a very short measure. The whole word "cheered" cannot be brought up to fill the first line because it is too long; "cheered" cannot be divided, so no part of it could be brought up. The best solution would be to letterspace the first line.

Richard M. Nixon
cheered the ball team.

The proofreader should try to fill a line of type in the beginning or middle of a paragraph whenever a change has made the line too short or too long. Otherwise the compositor will have to reset the entire paragraph, which is costly. (Similarly, in inserting or deleting a word to eliminate a "river of white" or

PROOFREADING   123

repeated words or hyphens, the proofreader should try to do so in the last lines, not in an early line that would necessitate resetting many succeeding lines.) For example:

The New York Mets Mets can be relied
upon to always do something that will
enthrall their fans.

The manuscript repeated the word "Mets," and it must be deleted on the galley. This would necessitate resetting all three lines, unless a word of comparable length was inserted in the first line. (Since space between words varies line by line, the proofreader can sometimes insert a longer word in a loose line, or a shorter word—or no word—in a tight line.) In this example the proofreader might insert "team" after "New York Mets." This would fill the line, so only one line would have to be changed. A margin note should be written to the publisher: "Ed: word inserted to fill line." Note: If the change is a PE— printer's error—the proofreader does *not* have to fiddle with these changes, for the compositor must assume the resetting costs.

A Brief Guide to Type

Type is available in a wide range of faces (styles), some suitable for close-packed columns in an encyclopedia, others so ornate they can be used only for emphasis in headlines. Type faces may be serif, with tiny finishing strokes on the top and bottom of each letter (as this type); or sans serif, straight up and down. Sizes vary from 5- and 6-point (a point is approximately 1/72 inch) to 144 points (about two inches), or even larger for earth-shaking newspaper headlines. A single typeface is usually available in roman lightface, roman boldface, italic lightface, and (sometimes) italic boldface. A single typeface also comes in many different sizes. One typeface in one size is called a font.

By carefully comparing the *t*'s, *r*'s, *y*'s, *c*'s, and *e*'s of two different samples of type, a layperson may be able to pinpoint the differences. It is much easier to see the differences if the same word is set in both typefaces.

A book designer chooses a basic text type and a display type (for chapter headings and similar stand-out material). The designer tells the compositor which typeface and size to use, and to what measure (width) the type is to be set.

The type used for the text of this book is 11/14 Plaideo Caledonia.[8]

The type used in this example
is 8/10 Caledonia, italics, boldface.

The type used in this example
is 9/10 Helvetica (sans serif), roman, regular.

A notation such as "11/14" (read "eleven on fourteen") means letters that are 11 points high with 3 points of leading between lines ($11 + 3 = 14$, the total height of the line). Similarly, 6/8 would mean 6-point letters with 2 points of leading ($6 + 2 = 8$).

Specialized training is needed to tell if the correct font has been used and the correct leading. But the proofreader should be alert for inconsistencies. (For example, too much leading, as between this line and

[8]The text of this edition (1979), which is an offset printing of the original, is slightly reduced.

the preceding one; and the wrong font, as the *t* in
"font.") The margin note by incorrect leading should
read: "Comp: note incorrect leading." The standard
marginal notation for the wrong font is "wf," plus a
circle drawn around the offending letter(s).

PROOFREADING COMPUTER PRINTOUTS

The latest wrinkle in printing is printing by computer. Original copy is coded and then fed into a computer, which provides a printout. Later, after all corrections have been made, the printout is fed back into the
computer and the computer is linked to a linotype.
Now computers are being geared also to do their own
proofreading.

Below is an example of a computer printout. The
letters enclosed in sideways carets are function codes
for the computer; they certainly will not be in the
finished book!

```
0046  old boxwood has been restored.º<IN>Open daily Mar.<OU>_<IN>Nov.? ı
0047  Mon.<OU>_<IN>Sat. Dec.<OU>_<IN>Feb. Small charge.<EP>ı
0048  )))ı
```

Just a few years ago function codes appeared for
many type elements, including capital letters, end-of-
line hyphens, and changes in type (as from roman to
italic or from lightface to boldface). Today's computers
are more sophisticated: Codes are normally suppressed
for capitalization and hyphens, and the proofreader can
actually see what will be printed. However, type
changes most often appear only as codes. And the type
may not be justified on the printout but may be coded
where lines will end.

The proofreader has to be aware of what the codes mean (the publisher should provide a list) and must check each and every one for accuracy. Judging from the experience of some freelancers who have proofread computer printouts, it is significantly harder work because the frequent codes confuse and compound the issue. The eyes suffer and the mind grows wearier with this type of proofreading. Freelancers who are asked to take on such a job should request a higher "hardship" rate for this work.

SUPPLIES AND BOOKS

SUPPLIES

Pencils of two different colors. The compositor's proofreader will use a certain color pencil, and the publisher's proofreader should use a different color.

Pencil sharpener (a good point is a must).

Tape (Scotch Magic Transparent Tape or Tuck Write-On Tape is best because it can be easily written on).

Typewriter (for retyping inserts and for preparing bills).

Typewriter paper (not the erasable kind . . . it smudges in handling).

BOOKS

The following books are listed in Appendix II, with all pertinent publishing information.

A proofreader must own Webster's dictionary. Webster's Seventh, the desk dictionary, will suffice,

although it is ideal to have Webster's Third Unabridged also . . . the unabridged is too cumber-
some to work with constantly.

Other useful books include:

A style manual (*Words into Type* and/or *A Manual of
Style*). It is difficult to resolve inconsistencies without having one or both of these to check the points
in dispute.

A good English grammar text (Strunk and White's
The Elements of Style is superb; Fowler's *Modern
English Usage* is a classic).

Atlas or gazetteer.

Current almanac.

A book delving deeply into the intricacies of proofreading (this one would be a good choice).

Also, to keep up-to-date with current events, a proofreader should regularly read a good newspaper. A
good news magazine is also helpful. The trade
publication *Publishers Weekly* will keep you
abreast of news in the world of publishing.

Chapter 5

INDEXING, FREELANCE

INDEXING is like eggplant: Freelancers either hate it or love it. Some of the freelancers replying to our questionnaire were quite outspoken. "I'd rather spend the whole day typing than ever do an index, even if indexing paid twice as well." "I do nothing but indexes—and I love it this way." How can the novice freelancer discover her own preferences without doing an index? And which publisher will assign her an index to do unless she has already done one?

If you are curious as to whether or not you would be any good at indexing and whether it would intrigue you or bore you stiff, read this chapter and try to index the samples on pages 135–136. Then index the entire money-tax chapter (Chapter 7) of this book and compare your index with the boldface entries in the index at the back of this book (all references to Chapter 7 are in boldface so that you can easily make the comparison).

You may be dismayed by the differences. Perhaps you have entries that are not included in the index; perhaps you omitted some that are included. Perhaps the page numbers on a given entry differ. But bear in mind that there is no such thing as a "perfect" index. If two—or three, or more—highly experienced and competent indexers were to index the same book, they would produce two—or three, or more—versions. Most of the differences would be in terminology. One would list under "money" what another would index under "cash" and yet a third list under "finances." None of these is necessarily incorrect.

The function of an index is to enable the reader to find what he is looking for. The *reader,* not the author or the indexer. Bear in mind when determining index entries not "where would *I* look to find this reference?" but "where would *the reader of this book* be likely to look?" Because indexes should be slanted to the reader's proclivities, authors generally are not good indexers of their own books (we hope this book is an exception). Thoroughly acquainted with the subject matter, authors may neglect cross-references that seem redundant or entries that seem simplistic to them. To *them,* but not necessarily to a reader approaching the subject for the first time, or even to another expert looking at the same subject with a different perspective (for example, a social worker consulting a book on inner-city neighborhoods written by a city planner).

Anyone who has ever tried to look up a generalized subject in a library card catalog or encyclopedia index has confronted the problem of "what is that classified under?" Perhaps she is trying to find information on farming techniques used to combat erosion. She checks "farming" in the encyclopedia. No entry. "Erosion." No entry. All the references listed under "agriculture" dismiss erosion in a sentence or two. Finally, under "soil," the information is un-earthed. An indexer should try to minimize this type problem, provided the space allotted for the index is sufficient to permit needed cross-references. The reader wants to read the book, not flounder through the index.

What is an index? A typical index alphabetically lists the names, places, facts, and theories presented in the text, and the pages where they are to be found. Of course index references must be condensed; otherwise the index would be as long as the text.

The actual mechanics of indexing are deceptively uncomplicated. The indexer reads the text pages or marked galleys through rapidly, and then a second time more slowly, circling or underlining words and phrases to be indexed, noting in the margin terms that should appear in the index that are not specifically mentioned in the text. Next she goes through the book a third time and writes the entries on index cards, probably revising her original marginal terms as she proceeds. She then alphabetizes her cards, if she has not been doing so as she goes along, and edits and organizes them. Next she types the index according to specifications provided by the pub-lisher. If necessary (alas, it always seems to be nec-essary), she deletes or combines entries to trim the index to its allotted length. Or she makes marginal check marks alongside those entries she feels are least essential, so the editor can cut the index down before or after it is set in type.

If indexing were just that, almost anyone could do it. But at nearly every stage the indexer must decide what to include and how the entries should read. Her decisions are based on her knowledge and past experiences of indexing and her own common sense.

PROFILE OF A SUCCESSFUL INDEXER

Basically, an indexer works methodically and pays careful attention to detail, has a broad general background and enough editorial expertise to edit and style her work, and—if the indexes she does are to be other than routine—is imaginative. Although reading indexes is not one of life's real joys, it is the best way to learn indexing.

She must have the patience to work slowly and the wit to understand what she is reading. Even a basic index of names and places cannot be done mechanically; the indexer must decide whether to list Lake George under *l* or *g;* whether to alphabetize New Jersey before or after Newark; whether a passing reference to the Rocky Mountains should be indexed at all. She must contend with an impatient editor or production department head who may display an amazing ignorance of how an index is compiled. One of the authors of this book, in the midst of a long indexing job, was asked by the editor, "What letter are you up to?" An indexer does not go through the entire book looking for words beginning with *a*, then with *b*, and so forth!

A successful indexer is a paradox: slow and patient but able to work under pressure of an early deadline (indexes, the last part of a book to be finished, are always rush jobs); methodical but imaginative; copying down entry after entry, page after page, but putting herself in both the author's place (what does she mean to say here?) and the readers' (where are they likely to look for this information?).

GETTING WORK AS AN INDEXER

Because of the length of time it takes to index a book—at least fifteen to twenty hours for every 100 book pages (including editing and typing)—and because indexing is always a rush job, a great majority of trade book publishers assign indexes to freelancers. The exceptions are usually done by the authors; in-house indexers are a real rarity. University press books, on the other hand, are far more commonly author-indexed.

There is a shortage of competent indexers, as some of the examples in this chapter, gleaned from actual indexes, prove only too well. Even a novice, if she does not advertise her status, can get assignments. This is one editorial job in which all prior experience must be freelance, since there is virtually no in-house indexing. Replies to this book's freelance survey bear this out; a substantial percentage of the full-time indexers had no publishing experience (although many were librarians).

The American Society of Indexers (235 Park Avenue South, 8th Floor, New York, N.Y. 10003) might be able to give the novice indexer some tips on getting started. Annual membership dues in the Society are $20 which includes a subscription to the *Indexer*. The *Indexer* is the journal of both the British and American indexing societies. A recent article explored the intriguing possibilities of copyrighted indexes—on which royal-

ties would be paid! The American Society of Indexers holds an annual all-day meeting in New York
City with lectures and workshops, and is attempting
to set up professional criteria for indexers and indexes.

Several indexing services are listed in the "Editorial Work—Free Lance" section of *Literary Market
Place*. These organizations may be looking for new
freelancers; get in touch with them. A course in basic
indexing techniques (see Appendix III) may give the
novice the training and confidence she needs to get
started.

After reading this chapter and indexing Chapter 7,
a determined person should be able to handle a simple index (one for a children's book would be perfect
for a start). A proofreader or copy editor could ask the
editor for whom she is doing a particular assignment
if she might do the index as well. Having read the
text through at least once, she would have that much
of an advantage when it came to starting the index.

The editor or production manager who gives the
assignment should provide the indexer with a set of
pages (or, more likely, cast-off galleys, which have
the page breaks marked in pencil) with proofreading
corrections marked. She should include specifications
for typing the index: the number of lines available,
the number of characters per line, and any particular
style the publisher wants. A few publishers accept
neatly written or typed index cards instead of a typed
manuscript. But generally the indexer must type the
index (or hire a typist, especially if typing numbers is
troublesome!). The copy editor's style sheet will help
when the time comes to copyedit the index.

Tools for indexing include 3 x 5 or 5 x 8 cards, ruled to help keep the page numbers straight. Most indexers, long familiar with library card catalogs, are more comfortable with the smaller size, although a lot more entries fit on the larger cards.

Cards can be used for more than one index by turning them upside down or flipping them over; it is best to write in different colored pen for each index, so that wrong entries will not be included. Cards bought by the thousand automatically provide another needed item: The box in which ten packs of 100 cards come is quite adequate for filing completed cards. A cardboard, wood, or metal file card box is also fine, but these may be too deep for easy filing.

Indexers also need alphabetical divider cards. These come with twenty-five or more subdivisions; sequentially tabbed blank cards are also available, if the indexer wants to make her own divisions. By using the latter the indexer can subdivide as finely as she likes; for a really massive index she might want to split the alphabet into 100 or more parts. And if she has a concentration of entries at one point (for example, the surname of the subject of a biography, with separate cards for his sisters and his cousins and his aunts), she can make more subdivisions there.

Colored pencils are necessary for marking the text pages, pens or pencils for making the index card entries, and paper and typewriter for typing the index manuscript. Some indexers prefer to type their cards, either on continuous-roll perforated cards or on regular cards. If using regular cards, place one in the typewriter in position to be typed on and place another just in the roller; in this way, rolling out the typed card will automatically roll the second card into position (five seconds saved). An established indexer might consider investing in a numbering machine (see Appendix II) to number the cards or typed pages.

Every indexer, novice or pro, needs a style guide to help with the tricky entries. Regular style manuals have sections on indexing; there are also indexing reference books available, which go into much more detail. These are listed in Appendix II.

TEXT REFERENCES

Before marking the text as a guide in making entries, all but the most experienced indexer should skim the index of another book on the same subject as the one being indexed. This will give an idea of what generic terms should be included and the particular problems of indexing that type of book. Back at her own text, the indexer must decide (1) which references are substantial enough to merit an index entry, (2) how these should be listed in the index, (3) what cross-references are needed, and (4) what generic references, for ideas discussed in the text but not explicitly cited, should be added.

What constitutes a reference? Here are some sample paragraphs. Decide what your index entries would be, and why, and then see the following lists of entries and reasons.

(A)   [p. 35] Throttlebottom, like such previous Vice Presidents as Laurel and Hardy, was handicapped by President Wintergreen's obvious reluctance to assign

him any significant role in the administration. Indeed
Mary Wintergreen, while ostensibly carrying out only
the largely ceremonial duties of the First Lady, was
considered by many a *de facto* Vice President. Even
after the Samovar Mound scandal discredited Ms.
Wintergreen and her protégé, the Secretary of State,
the President kept the lid on Throttlebottom.

(B)   [p. 173] Constructing a better mousetrap may not in-
duce the world to beat a path to your door; hopefully
though it will enable you to control your rodent problem. For this trap you will need 6 pieces of ¾-inch
plywood 6 x 10 inches, a 9 x 5 x ½-inch board, a
5-inch length of ¾-inch dowel, heavy-duty twine,
a screw eye, and 1½-inch common nails. With a rab-
bet plane or backsaw, cut grooves ¾-inch wide ½
inch from the end of two plywood pieces. [p. 174]
The grooves should run down the short (6-inch) sides.
In the same pieces, make ¾-inch grooves ½ inch
from one long edge, crossing the shorter grooves (see
Fig. 1).

(C)   [p. 13] It was at Peter Pan School in 1377 that young
Henry Percy first met his cousin, Prince Henry, who
was to have such a great impact on the future course
of his life. Other schoolmates included Dicky Scroop,
a happy-go-lucky youngster whose devil-may-care
behavior gave no hint of his future vocation as a
churchman and Archbishop of York; impetuous
Owen "Taffy" Glendower; Dick Vernon; Jack
"Chubby" Falstaff; Ned Poins; and Eddie Mortimer.
Ironically, little Mortimer, a sworn enemy of Percy's
in school days, was later to become his brother-in-
law, while cousin Henry was Percy's inseparable
chum at school.

(A)   Doe, John Q. (1852–1920), 35
First Lady, role of, 35
Hardy, Andrew (1930–   ), 35
Laurel, Stanley (1797–1883), 35
Presidency, U.S., 35

Samovar Mound Scandal of 1916, 35
State, Secretary of, 35
Throttlebottom, Alexander (1858–1917), 35
Turner, Mary, *see* Wintergreen, Mary Turner
Vice President, role of, 35
Wintergreen, John (1850–1930), 35
Wintergreen, Mary Turner (1870–1945), 35

Notice that the indexer has added information not in the text (some of it would doubtless be found on other pages), such as first names, maiden names, full names of persons mentioned only by title (i.e., John Doe, the erstwhile Secretary of State). Indexers should always try to fill in missing names, but they must do so as carefully as they index! Our hypothetical indexer has, in one instance, made things worse. Instead of writing a note to the editor, asking him or the author to provide former Vice President Hardy's first name, she has consulted a biographical dictionary, but emerged with the wrong Hardy: a living Andrew rather than Oliver (1750–1828). Better to give no information than the *wrong* information.

An indexer may be asked to supply additional details such as dates of birth and death, or reigns (for monarchs and ecclesiastics). If the indexer has not been asked to provide these details but believes, after her first reading of the text, that such information would be of great use to the reader, she should call the editor and suggest it. Since additions take more time to research, and since the indexer's time is the publisher's money, she should not go ahead without inquiring first.

Entries such as those for former Vice Presidents Hardy and Laurel are moot, since they are referred to only in passing. Some indexers believe these casual mentions are not substantial enough to merit index references; others feel impelled to index every person mentioned in the text—even if only listed in passing in a long string of names. If all names are included, the indexer may be forced to sacrifice references to events or ideas in order to make the index fit the space available. In this particular case, since parallels are set up among the three Veeps, one might argue that there is "information" provided about Laurel and Hardy; that they, like Throttlebottom, were allowed no great roles in their administrations.

If the text dealt exclusively with the Presidency and Vice Presidency, such references might be redundant. In a 475-page book entitled *The Vice President: A Choice or an Echo,* an entry such as: Vice President, role of, 1–475, would be nonsensical.

(B) backsaw, 173
     dowel, 173
     eye, screw, 173
     groove, cutting, 173–174 (*or* 173–74 *or* 173–4)
     mousetrap, building, 173–174
     nail, common, 173
     plane, rabbet, 173
     plywood, 173
     saw, 00, 000, 000; *see also* backsaw
     twine, heavy-duty, 173

Did you spot the change of page numbers halfway through the paragraph? An indexer must stay alert! One of the commonest indexing errors, especially after the indexer has been working for several hours, is to mechanically continue to enter "173" on the cards after she reaches page 174.

Example (B) is an extremely detailed list of entries. Conceivably, the entire paragraph could be represented by: mousetrap, building, 173–174. (Note the different ways of styling numbers.) Cross-indexing compound words such as backsaw or jackhammer helps the reader.

(C)   Douglas, Archibald, 13
      Falstaff, John, 13
      Glendower, Owen, 13
      Henry IV, King of England: childhood, 13
      Mortimer, Edmund, 13
      Percy, Henry
        childhood, 13
      Peter Pan School (Windsor, England), 13
      Poins, Edward, 13
      Scroop, Richard, 13
      Vernon, Richard, 13
      York, Archbishop of, *see* Scroop, Richard

For a biography, entries for the subject and for others mentioned many times should be subdivided, both to avoid long strings of numbers and to avoid a ridiculous entry such as: Percy, Henry, 1–350. Note the different ways subentries can be listed (as in the Henry IV and Percy, Henry, entries in the example above). Some publishers have definite style preferences; others do not care as long as the index is internally consistent.

Deciding how entries should be listed is mostly a matter of common sense. People are listed under their last names; books by their titles, with beginning articles inverted; common nouns by the key word; organizations generally by the key word. For example:

Donne, John
Canterbury Tales, The
birch, yellow
State, Department of

The exceptions make an indexer's life interesting.
Study the following and decide how you would enter
them in an index, then compare with the lists that
follow. Hint: In some cases more than one entry may
be needed. Think of the key word(s).

Napoleon Bonaparte
Dick Van Dyke, Ludwig van Beethoven, Vincent van
    Gogh
Charles de Gaulle, Victoria de los Angeles, Henri de
    Toulouse-Lautrec
Eliot Fremont-Smith, Ralph Vaughan Williams, David
    Lloyd George (the Earl of Dufor)
John Churchill (the First Duke of Marlborough)
Anne Boleyn
Mark Twain, O. Henry, Imamu Amiri Baraka
Mao Tse-tung, Chung Hee Park, Eisaku Sato
Omar Khayyám, Ahmed Ben Bella, David Ben Gurion

sugar maples, maple sugar
Baseball Hall of Fame, Brooklyn Dodgers
National Council of Education, American Association of
    University Professors (AAUP)
The Gold Coast, Africa
dialectical materialism, abstract expressionism
Church of Jesus Christ of Latter-day Saints

Indexing names, especially Islamic, African, Asian,
double-barreled British, and Spanish, is less simple
than it may seem. A good style manual (*Manual of
Style* or *Words into Type*) will provide some tips for

names, especially unfamiliar ones where the indexer may not be sure which is the surname and which the personal name (or what word, in fact—such as "U" in Burmese—is equivalent to "Ms." or "Mr." in a particular language). Of course the stylistically correct listing is not necessarily where people will look; the indexer should anticipate the reader and cross-index likely references.

TEXT	INDEX
Napoleon Bonaparte	Napoleon Bonaparte
	Bonaparte, Napoleon, *see* Napoleon Bonaparte
Dick Van Dyke, Ludwig van Beethoven, Vincent van Gogh	Van Dyke, Dick
	Beethoven, Ludwig van
	Van Gogh, Vincent
	Gogh, Vincent van, *see* Van Gogh, Vincent
Charles de Gaulle, Victoria de los Angeles, Henri de Toulouse-Lautrec	De Gaulle, Charles
	De los Angeles, Victoria
	Toulouse-Lautrec, Henri de
Eliot Fremont-Smith, Ralph Vaughan Williams, David Lloyd George (the Earl of Dufor)	Fremont-Smith, Eliot
	Vaughan Williams, Ralph
	Williams, Ralph Vaughan, *see* Vaughan Williams, Ralph
	Lloyd George, David
	Dufor, Earl of, *see* Lloyd George, David
	George, David Lloyd, *see* Lloyd George, David
John Churchill (the First Duke of Marlborough)	Marlborough, First Duke of (John Churchill)
	Churchill, John, *see* Marlborough, First Duke of

TEXT	INDEX
Anne Boleyn	Boleyn, Anne
	Anne Boleyn, Queen of England, *see* Boleyn, Anne
Mark Twain, O. Henry, Imamu Amiri Baraka	Twain, Mark, *see* Clemens, Samuel Langhorne
	O. Henry, *see* Porter, William Sydney
	Henry, O., *see* Porter, William Sydney
	Baraka, Imamu Amiri, *see also* Jones, LeRoi
	Imamu Amiri Baraka, *see* Baraka, Imamu Amiri
	Amiri Baraka, Imamu, *see* Baraka, Imamu Amiri
Mao Tse-tung, Chung Hee Park, Eisaku Sato	Mao Tse-tung
	Park, Chung Hee
	Sato, Eisaku
Omar Khayyám, Ahmed Ben Bella, David Ben Gurion	Omar Khayyám
	Khayyám, Omar, *see* Omar Khayyám
	Bella, Ahmed Ben
	Ben Gurion, David

Some general rules and the reasons for some exceptions: In general, the equivalent of "of" (van, de, della) is ignored in indexing. Strictly speaking, the French general and politician should be listed under "Gaulle, Charles de." But who would look for his name there? And if a person is referred to in both ways, such as Vincent van Gogh, it is best to make two entries. As for the English people, the hyphens are not always present in double-barreled names. A biographical dictionary is helpful in making such determinations. The contradiction between the Lloyd George and the Churchill listings is explained by common sense: Lloyd George is universally known by his surname; the first Churchill is known as the Duke of Marlborough. Similarly, while Anne Boleyn is listed under her maiden name, her father-in-law, Henry Tudor, would be listed as Henry VII of England, with a cross-reference from his family name. Pseudonyms should refer the reader to the original name, but someone who takes a new name should be listed under that name, with a reference to his or her former name; in a chronological work there might be references under both present and previous names, with the person's second name in parentheses: Muhammad Ali (Cassius Clay) for example.

Asian, African, and Arabic names follow their own rules. The family name comes first in Chinese names. Korean names may either start with the family name, Chinese style, or end with it, Western style: Chung Hee Park was formerly known as Park Chung Hee. Arabic names are usually indexed under the personal name (Omar the Tentmaker, Ahmed the son of Bella), except for Westernized names, such as that of former Algerian premier Ahmed Ben Bella. Note that "Ben" in Arabic names is the equivalent of "de" or "van"; in Hebrew names it is part of the surname.

If a name is totally baffling and the indexer cannot locate it in a reference book, she should query the editor. The author *should* know.

TEXT	INDEX
sugar maples, maple sugar	maples, sugar
	sugar, maple
Baseball Hall of Fame,	Hall of Fame, Baseball

TEXT	INDEX
Brooklyn Dodgers	Dodgers, Brooklyn
	Brooklyn Dodgers, *see* Dodgers, Brooklyn
National Council of Education, American Association of University Professors (AAUP)	Education, National Council of
	University Professors, American Association of
	Professors, American Association of University, *see* University Professors, American Association of
	AAUP, *see* University Professors, American Association of
The Gold Coast, Africa dialectical materialism, abstract expressionism	Gold Coast, Africa, *see* Ghana
	materialism, dialectical
	expressionism, abstract
	abstract expressionism, *see* expressionism, abstract
Church of Jesus Christ of Latter-day Saints	Church of Jesus Christ . .
	Latter-day Saints, *see* Church of . . .
	Mormons, *see* Church of Jesus Christ . . .

Think of the key word when indexing an organization or concept, especially in a book aimed at the general reader. Educators are doubtless familiar with the National Council of Education; lay people will miss the reference unless it is indexed or cross-indexed under "education." Similarly with the AAUP. Organizations like AA, AAA, and NAACP are best indexed under the familiar initials, with the full name in parentheses, and, if there is sufficient space, a cross-reference at "Alcoholics Anonymous," "American

Automobile Association," and "National Association for the Advancement of Colored People."

Use common sense. In a book about baseball it makes no sense to index "Baseball Hall of Fame" under the first word. The same book included listings for "Brooklyn Dodgers" and "Los Angeles Dodgers," but none for "Dodgers."

Names of countries change—sometimes midway in the text—watch out for them (see page 38 in the copyediting chapter).

Cross-index when in doubt . . . if there is sufficient space to do so. Page entries should be under the most logical reference, even if not the strictly correct one. Then if cross-references are deleted, at least the entries will be in the likeliest place.

Cross-references lead the reader from synonyms to the main entry, from one entry to a parallel one, from a subdivision to the main entry. Page numbers should be listed in both places for single-line entries, as in "corn" and "maize" in the following list. However, cross-references for long entries ("money" and "finances") should refer the reader to the most likely word.

corn, 622
evolution, 99
   see also selection, natural
finances, 68, 92, 133
   corporate, 162–64
   personal, 141–45
maize, 622
money, *see* finances
selection, natural, 197–208
   see also evolution

Cross-references are also needed because of style variations. If a book refers to the cities of München and Bruxelles, then that is how they should appear in the index. Naturally the indexer would add the cross-references "Munich, *see* München" and "Brussels, *see* Bruxelles." Backsaws, hacksaws, and jigsaws should be under *b*, *h*, and *j*. Since crosscut saws, circular saws, and such will be listed under *s*, the main "saws" entry should include a cross-reference.

saws, 99–106
  see also backsaw; hacksaw; jigsaw

The indexer should not go overboard on cross-referencing and thereby lead the reader on a wild goose chase. Nothing is more infuriating than:

golf, *see* games

And when the reader gets to "games":

games
  golf, 23, 57

(If there are only a few entries, why not list them under "golf" instead of a cross-reference?)
  Nothing is more infuriating, that is, unless it is:

whistler, *see* woodchuck
woodchuck, *see* marmot

The most difficult entries are for ideas, especially ideas not explicitly stated in the text. This is where an indexer's skill, intelligence, and care are essential.

The first reading acquaints the indexer with the ideas expressed in the text. The second time through she must mark them in the margins. Sometimes an author will state an idea or describe a concept explicitly in an early chapter, then refer to it later in a somewhat offhand manner. (Sometimes, if the editor has not done her job, an idea will be casually referred to in an early chapter and then expounded toward the end of the book!) The indexer's job is to catch those offhand references. When making generic references, as when indexing names, she should choose the most likely term: hunters rather than predators; gardening rather than horticulture; leaves rather than foliage. Of course this rule would not apply to a scientific or technical work.

As the indexer goes through the galleys or pages, marking index entries, she should keep a list of the general terms. This will remind her to continue looking for them throughout the book. This also deters her from indexing relevant references under "hunter" in the first half of the book and under "predator" in the second half—and never getting the references assembled in one place. Here are some sample paragraphs and the generic references that might be made for them. Notice that the type of reference depends very definitely on the book being indexed.

SCIENCE TEXT:

That time of year thou mayst in me behold, when yellow leaves, or none, or few, do hang upon those boughs which shake against the cold, bare ruin'd choirs, where late the sweet birds sang.

INDEX ENTRIES:

abscission layer
autumn
carotene
migration, bird

PSYCHOLOGY TEXT:

That time of year thou mayst in me behold, when yellow leaves, or none, or few, do hang upon those boughs which shake against the cold, bare ruin'd choirs, where late the sweet birds sang.

INDEX ENTRIES:

aging, attitudes to-
    ward
  of aging people
  of others
aging, physiolog-
    ical signs of
    balding

HISTORY OF TUDOR ENGLAND TEXT:

That time of year thou mayst in me behold, when yellow leaves, or none, or few, do hang upon those boughs which shake against the cold, bare ruin'd choirs, where late the sweet birds sang.

choirs, boy
monasteries
    closed by Henry
    VIII
    treasures confis-
    cated
schools, church
    closed by Henry
    VIII

POLITICAL SCIENCE TEXT:

When in the course of human events it becomes necessary for one people to dissolve the political bands which have connected them with another, and to assume among the powers of the earth the separate and equal station to which the laws of nature and of nature's God entitle them, a decent respect for the opinions of mankind requires that they should declare the causes which impel them to the separation.

colonies
governments, Eu-
    ropean
history, political
public opinion
revolution, causes
    of

Making Entries

There are two schools of thought concerning index card entries (examples on page 150). School A teaches: Make a separate card for each reference, toss into a shoebox, then sort and alphabetize and combine the cards. School B, whose proponents cannot face the thought of alphabetizing wads of cards at one sitting, advises: File each card in alphabetical order right after it is written; then check each underlined (or marginally noted) phrase against completed cards to see if there has been a previous reference. If so, add the new page number to the existing card. If not, make up a card and file it. The advantage of this system is that after the last page is indexed, the index is already alphabetized and ready for editing.

An annex to School B employs a simpler method, but one that often is ultimately more frustrating. As the entries come up, they are noted on sheets of paper or in a thumb-indexed notebook. It requires great expertise to know in advance how much space each letter will take. And even if the indexer judges correctly letter by letter, she may wind up with a confused jumble on a legal-size page, with "axes" at the top right corner and "acorns" at the bottom. A very real danger is that page numbers from one entry will run into numbers from another (this could also happen if she tries to squeeze main entries and all subentries on the same index card).

Do not index without thinking. The original index for a nature book had no entry for prairie dogs. It turned out the indexer had put the page references under "dogs." Not even under "dogs, prairie" (these little burrowers are actually ground squirrels)—but

Doe, John Q., 10

Doe, John Q., 28

Doe, John Q., 35

Doe, John Q., $42\frac{1}{N}43$

SCHOOL A

Doe, John Q., 10, 28, 35, $42\frac{1}{N}43$

SCHOOL B

under dogs, period. Watch out for the prairie dogs, guinea pigs, and Bombay duck! If readers might look under the common noun, the cross-references should read:

"dogs," prairie, *see* prairie dogs
"pigs," guinea, *see* guinea pigs
"duck," Bombay, *see* fish, dried salted

Also watch for homonyms or identical proper names. These must be differentiated in the entries:

bookmaking (betting)
bookmaking (publishing)

Humperdinck, Engelbert (German composer)
Humperdinck, Engelbert (singer)

magazines (ammunition)
magazines (periodicals)

Be careful of page number listings. The entries 96, 97 imply two separate references on those pages; 96–97 implies a continuous discussion. If pressed for space, a string of separate but adjoining page numbers—23, 24, 25, 26, 27—may be combined (23–27) rather than deleting the reference entirely. The references should be kept separate, however, until after the index is typed to measure and the length can be more accurately determined. It is easier to condense an index than to try to expand it.

Page numbers for illustrations are usually boldfaced or italicized; maps are sometimes italicized. The publisher may ask that the "main entry" be boldfaced. Whatever key is used, it should be clearly explained at the beginning of the index as a guide to readers.

SUBENTRIES

As the indexer marks the galleys, she should consider which entries should be subdivided and should make as many subentries as possible. Later, if the typed index runs too long, she can always condense, eliminate the subentries, and add those page numbers to the main entry. To have to go back through the book to try to subdivide an entry with a long string of numbers is annoying, at best. It is so much easier to do it right from the beginning.

Subentries can mean the difference between a useful and a useless index. A recent best-selling historical biography has a truly appalling index. Several major figures have index entries consisting of a name followed by *twenty or more lines* of page numbers. Faced with such an entry a reader might as well just read through the whole book. To someone doing research, with a score of books to consult, such entries rule out that biography as a source, for who has the time to sift through 200-plus pages to find the reference to one incident?

Since an index is not an outline, an entry need not have two or more subentries; one is perfectly acceptable, if it works out that way.

Wilson, Woodrow, 75–94
    as President, 88–91

Remember that subentries must truly be *part* of the larger topic. A book on St. Bernards had the following:

dogs
    circulatory systems, 23
    drooling, 17
    evolution, 48
    food, 27
    houses, 13–15
    trainers, 12, 14–16

Two points here. First, the "drooling" referred to a discussion of Pavlov's experiments with salivation. The word "drooling" never appeared in the text! As noted previously, when discussing generic terms it is fine to try to think of more popular terms under which the reader is likely to look. But do not get too colloquial. Second, dog food, dog houses, and dog trainers are not parts of dogs; circulatory systems, salivation, and evolution are. As revised, the entries read (the alphabetization will be explained later):

dog food, 27
dog houses, 13–15
dogs
    circulatory systems, 23
    evolution, 48
    reflexes, 17
    salivation, 17
dog trainers, 12, 14–16

In making subentries, just as in making generic entries, watch out for two differently worded phrases meaning the same thing, especially if they have different sets of page numbers:

goods   furniture
    commercial expense, 215   bureaus, 24
    purchase and sale, 187–195   couches, 8–9

retail cost of, 322
sale and purchase, 217–222

dressers, 17
sofas, 26–31

Embarrassing for the indexer and totally confusing for the reader!

And just as main entries should be alphabetized under the commonest nouns or key words, so should the subentries.

WRONG	RIGHT
accidents, automobile	accidents, automobile
caused by minor driver	minor driver, caused by
filing report	prevention of
how to prevent	reports, filing
marriage	marriage
duties toward in-laws	children, role of
role of children	in-laws, duties toward

Do not index according to adjectives and adverbs. Delete excessive prepositions (ignore them in the alphabetization in any case) but leave them in titles and where needed for meaning.

love
  function of, in marriage
  of puppies

The "of" in the first subentry could be deleted; the second should be retained to avoid confusion.

SUB-SUBENTRIES

There is no stylistic reason to avoid sub-subentries, or even sub-sub-subentries, but there is an aesthetic one. Indexes are generally set on a narrow column no more than forty characters wide. Sub-subentries must be indented four characters, and runover lines eight characters. Sub-sub-subentries need indentions of six and ten characters. Such short lines have a choppy look. Of course, if subdivisions are needed, they may be used, as in this example. (The alphabetization under "education" will be explained later.)

Einstein, Albert
  education
      gymnasium, 17–23
      college, 23–37
      graduate school, 36–48
  writings
      on mathematics, 77, 85–102
      on philosophy
          Why War?, 109, 115, 133–138,
              145, 167, 177, 192, 195,
              210–215
          World As I See It, The, 110,
              115, 133–138, 245

Such entries could be handled differently by reorganizing the main topic:

Einstein, Albert, education of
    gymnasium, 17–23
    college, 23–37
    graduate school, 36–48
Einstein, Albert, works by
    on mathematics, 77, 85–102
    on philosophy, *see Why War?;*
        World As I See It, The

ALPHABETIZING AND EDITING

There are two methods of alphabetizing, both equally "correct." Unless the publisher specifies a certain method (or the author, in organizing material in the text, has clearly favored one method), the indexer can choose whether to alphabetize letter-by-letter or word-by-word. In letter-by-letter, everything up to the first comma (ignoring apostrophes, dashes, and hyphens) is considered as one run-on series of letters. In word-by-word, the first word of the entry is considered, then the next, etc.; the rule is "nothing (a space between words is nothing) precedes something (a letter)." Although it might seem that there would be little difference between the two, consider these examples:

LETTER-BY-LETTER	WORD-BY-WORD
dog houses	dog houses
dogs	dog trainers
dog trainers	dogs

"Dogs" come before "dog trainers" in the letter-by-letter method because *s* comes before *t*; "dogs" come last in the word-by-word method because *nothing* (the space after "dog" in the "dog trainers" entry) *precedes something* (the final *s* in "dogs"). Similarly:

LETTER-BY-LETTER	WORD-BY-WORD
Newfoundland	New Haven
New Haven	New Jersey
New Jersey	New York State
Newport	*New Yorker*
New Yorker	Newfoundland
New York State	Newport

Letter-by-letter alphabetizing is used in the index of this book.

Some miscellaneous points: "Mc" is usually indexed as though it were spelled "Mac." But the New York Telephone book, and some other strictly letter-by-letter indexes, place the "Mc"s after MBZ Enterprises. "St." for "Saint" should be treated as though it were spelled out—whether or not it is. The same rule applies to Mr., Dr., and such, in the unlikely event that these occur at the beginning of an entry (they might proliferate if you were indexing a book on films: "Mister Roberts," "Doctor Kildare"). Numbers are treated as though they were spelled out (4-H Clubs under *f*, *20,000 Leagues Under the Sea* under *t*).

There is even an order of precedence for listing identically worded entries:

John (saint)
John (pope)
John (emperor)
John (king)
John (prince)
John (peer)
John (personal name)
John, Chester (surname)
John, Alabama (place)
john, *see* bathroom (subject)
John (title)

Initials should be indexed according to what they stand for, not by themselves. However, if the acronym is so well known that most people have forgotten the exact wording of the original, index under the initials; i.e., "NATO" after "nation," and "SCUBA" after "science," but "IBM," spelled out as "International Business Machines," after "international affairs" rather than just after "iambic." Sometimes the name of a foundation or museum will include the entire name of the donor; this should be indexed strictly alphabetically, *not* under the donor's last name. For example:

Henrietta, Queen of England
Henry E. Huntington Library
Horney, Karen

metals
M. H. de Young Memorial Museum
minerals

If space permits, there should be a cross-reference or separate entry under "Huntington" and "de Young."

There are quite a few variations in the way an index may be edited and styled, in the way subentries are listed, in the way numbers are listed, in the way cross-references are treated. Generally the indexer is on her own and can follow her own wishes. One basic difference is whether subentries are run in or are on separate lines. As can be seen from the following examples, the space requirements of the two basic styles are quite different—a point to bear in mind when space is tight.

CONDENSED STYLE
cats: breeds, 22; eating habits, 17–20; fur, 96; markings, 34–35

OPEN STYLE
cats
　breeds, 22
　eating habits, 17–20
　fur, 96
　markings, 34–35

In addition, the first letter of each main entry can be capitalized or lowercased. Subentries are usually lowercased.

A major departure from alphabetical listing is to list certain entries or subentries in chronological or numerical order. For example:

Henry I
Henry II
Henry III
Henry IV
Henry V

Going in strict alphabetical order—which would be nonsensical in this case—the list would read:

Henry V (the Fifth)
Henry I (the First)
Henry IV (the Fourth)
Henry II (the Second)
Henry III (the Third)

In addition, subentries are sometimes listed in chronological rather than alphabetical order, especially where they refer to the subject of a biography. If this is done, it should be consistent in parallel cases throughout the index.

ALPHABETICAL	CHRONOLOGICAL

Edward VIII,
    King of England
	Edward VIII,
	    King of England

abdication	birth
birth	education
coronation	coronation
death	abdication
education	marriage
marriage	death

There are two choices in styling inclusive numbers: 118–129 *or* 118–29. The tens indicator can even be dropped if it remains the same: 101–5 rather than 101–105 or 101–05. This very abbreviated method can be confusing,' however; it is best to avoid it. If a style is established in the book (as for page references), it should probably be followed in the index, as should the alphabetizing style. Note that en dashes are used to separate page numbers.

There are two choices in styling inclusive numbers: 118–129 *or* 118–29. The tens indicator can even be dropped if it remains the same: 101–5 rather than 101–105 or 101–05. This very abbreviated method can be confusing, however; it is best to avoid it. If a style is established in the book (as for page references), it should probably be followed in the index, as should the alphabetizing style. Note that en dashes are used to seperate page numbers.

Punctuation in indexes depends upon the style. In open style, usually neither the main nor subentries are separated by punctuation marks. In the run–in condensed style, a main entry with no page numbers is usually followed by a colon; semicolons seperate subentries (and also follow a main entry *with* page numbers). Entry blocks (main plus subs) in both styles generally have *no* terminal punctuation. Some publishers/authors have decided style preferences (or eccentricities); be sure to check. (A publisher may assume that you "know" the house index style.)

A miniature index, typed in both the open style and the condensed style, appears on the following pages.

INDEX

Boldface numbers refer to illustrations

Abercorn, Earl of, see Hamilton, James

Acton, Sir John

birth, 10

education, 12-14

military career in Naples, 13, 15-17, 16

prime minister of Naples, 16, 18

retirement in Sicily, 18-20, 18

death, 10, 18, 20

Adam, Robert, 14, 107-108, 233-237

Adams style, 108-110

Adrian IV, 152

see also Breakspear, Nicholas

Africa, colonial snobbery in, 238, 297-303,

378, 385, 442

see also individual countries

Albert, Prince

birth, 321

education, 321-323

travels, 322, 370

marriage, 322, 341

as prince consort, 341-359

death, 359

Amherst, Baron Jeffrey, 72, 85

Anne (Stuart), Queen of England, 12-14

Arbuthnot, John, 96-108

Bacon, Sir Francis, 17, 85, 227, 234, 302-303

□□371, 432, 515

⊓birth, 123

education, 122-124

political career, 122-127

literary works, 13, 125, 374

philosophical works, 13, 125, 372-375

banishment, 128

pardon, 128

death, 129

Austen House
Bennett: SNOBS AND SUPERSNOBS

Susan Laurens
2080 Madison Avenue, NYC

INDEX

Boldface numbers refer to illustrations

A few random comments about the preceding indexes: Although the indexer does not have to mark indentions (2 ems for runovers of main entries, 1 em for subentries, 3 ems for subentry runovers) throughout, it is not a bad idea. If the first subentry occurs at the top of a new page it should definitely be marked. Just as in typing any manuscript, avoid word breaks at the end of a line. But also try to avoid consistently typing a character or two over measure, for it will be difficult to judge the true number of lines. If the line is nearly all numerals, the compositor may be able to squeeze in an extra character or two, but this is difficult to do with letters.

The different kinds of "see also" references can also affect the length of the index:

tools, 17–25
　see also drill; hammer; saw;
　　screwdriver; wrench

tools, 17–25
　see also specific tools

(Note that general "see also" references are usually italicized along with the "see also" notation; specific references are not italicized.)

Do not forget the line space between *a* and *b* entries, and so forth: a maximum of twenty-five lines, but if space is running tight on a short index, that can make quite a difference.

If the index must be cut and the indexer just cannot decide what should go, she should indicate in the margin those entries the editor can delete with the least qualms. (An index should never run much shorter than requested by the publisher.)

Any queries about first names, dual spellings, etc., should also be noted in the margin of the typed index or on copyediting flags. Inconsistencies or errors within the text should be brought to the editor's attention in a separate memo, listing the specific page or galley numbers. Do not be surprised at finding errors. Even the best copy editor occasionally nods; or the error may be a printer's goof, which is often not corrected on the indexer's set of page proofs (a bad practice). The indexer must proofread the finished index as carefully as humanly possible.

SPECIALIZED INDEXES

Some of the problems of indexing a biography have been discussed previously. Cookbook indexes—which are basically straightforward—may include translations if the names are in a foreign language, or a listing of recipes by main ingredient or type of dish. For example:

stews
   bouillabaisse, 237
   goulash, 418
   gumbo, 478
swordfish
   Broiled Fish Delights, 285

Books of poetry, especially anthologies, generally have three separate indexes: authors, titles, and first lines. Infrequently these are combined in one alphabetical list, with the titles in quotation marks and the first lines in italics to set them off. In first-line indexes, an article is *not* dropped from the beginning of the line:

The bird is lost, 58
The glory of the day was in her face, 15
These were our fields, 31

If the first line is only one word long, or the phrase quoted makes a different sense from that intended by the poem, quote more:

Down/Down into the fathomless depths, 94
I/Have Arrived, 92

Always follow the author's capitalization and punctuation exactly as written.

COMPUTER INDEXING

An indexer must be a paradox of virtues: methodical and imaginative, patient and fastworking. It seems impossible that a machine could do such work—but more and more, indexes are being done by computer, especially indexes for encyclopedias and other extremely long and involved technical works. Of course there is a catch: An experienced indexer must carefully mark the galleys, keying entries for the computer. Different codes are used to "tell" the computer when to make a subentry, what to boldface or italicize. Then the computer does—infinitely faster than any team of indexers could—the equivalent of going through the book and noting the entries on cards.

The rough index produced by a computer must still be alphabetized and edited by an experienced editor, who can make the value judgments a computer cannot. Here is an example of the type of index a computer would produce:

Abercorn, Earl of, 57, 99
Abercorn, Earl of, *see* Hamilton, James
Abercorn, Earl James, 57, 99
Acton, John Francis (soldier)
  military career in Naples, 13, 15–17
Acton, John Francis Edward (statesman)
  prime minister of Naples, 16, 18
  retirement in Sicily, 18–20
Acton, Sir John (Brit. officer)
  birth, 10
  education, 12–14
  death, 10, 18, 20

The computer cannot recognize that all the James Abercorns and John Actons are the same men. If some references to the German saint were under Adalbert and some under Adelbert, they might not be combined (unless the indexer who keyed for the computer noted the cross-reference). Computers can eliminate the drudgery of indexing but will not replace, at least in the foreseeable future, the quixotic human element.

Try indexing Chapter 7. Good luck!

Chapter 6

DOTTING THE I's,
CROSSING THE T's,
TRANSLATING FROM CANTONESE

More and more, jobs that were once the prerogative of (publishing)-house-bound employees are being handled by freelancers. A publisher could hire one acquisitions editor (or deal with authors and agents himself) and farm out *all* editorial and production work: manuscript evaluating, translating, typing, manuscript editing, designing, copyediting, proofreading, picture research or editing, dummying, page proofing, indexing, jacket design, and flap-copy writing. Such a publisher could operate from a one-room office—some actually do—saving enormous amounts on overhead, salaries during slack periods, and employee benefits. Freelancers are helped because ever more assignments are available (although if publishers closed down existing editorial departments, there would also be more editorial personnel competing for work).

The design of a book, and its cover and jacket, cannot be divorced from the book's editorial content (not if the designer is sensitive to the nuances of an experimental novel, a sensational exposé, the pompous memoirs of a long-retired politician), but the following brief survey does not include the field of art and design. There are opportunities enough just in editorial work!

MANUSCRIPT TYPING

One of the few freelance jobs open to those with absolutely no experience in publishing, typing is an excellent way to start out. Even if you are a slow typist—although you must not be a sloppy one—and therefore do not make very much money (typing is paid by the page, so the faster you type the more you earn), the experience will prepare you for proofreading assignments. And since typing can be done page by page in short sessions, it is ideal work for a homemaker with importunate children (unlike copyediting and indexing, which require long, uninterrupted work sessions).

The publisher may ask that the manuscript be typed to a specific character count per line. If no specifications are given, leave top, bottom, and side margins of at least an inch: Pity the editor and copy editor who will have to write notes and queries in those margins later. *Always* double space (unless the publisher asks for triple spacing). Any standard typewriter, pica or elite, is acceptable—but that italic script, which flows so elegantly on your pseudo-handwritten personal letters, is out. Also verboten are ribbon-ink colors other than black, paper other than plain white bond. Do not go to the expense of stocking up on vellum or erasable paper. One is an extravagance and the other is actually undesirable. The pages you type will be handled later by at least five people: the editor, author, copy editor, compositor, and proofreader. Erasable paper smudges, so by the time the proofreader gets the pages, they may be unreadable. To correct typing errors you can use strike-over Ko-rec-type, Liquid Paper correction fluid, or tape that is pasted over the error. The tape is essential if you are typing camera copy, which must be perfect since it is actually photographed. Ordinary manuscripts need not be pristine.

Type the manuscript exactly as you receive it (making any changes marked, of course), except for correcting misspelled words. Even here, proceed with caution. A novelist may deliberately misspell to emphasize a character's illiteracy; the author may be using a perfectly acceptable alternate spelling with which you are unacquainted; an English or Anglophilic writer may make a practise of spelling honour and theatre just that way. Let the editor and copy editor question the author; it is their job.

By all means, though, make a list of your queries and send them to the editor along with the manuscript. Even if the editor decides to discount your recommendations, you will have demonstrated your alertness and perhaps your ability to move on to proofreading and copyediting.

Some special typing problems may come up. Do not hyphenate the last word on a line. Doing so will make extra work for you (checking a dictionary to make sure you are syllabicating properly) and later, for the copy editor (checking to make sure you *did*

syllabicate properly). Brackets should not be re-
placed by parentheses; type a slash plus two under-
scores [ ] or draw in by hand. To indicate a British
pound sign, type a hyphen over a capital "L." Turn
your carriage up a half space [1] for a superscript or
down a half space [2] for a subscript. Footnotes may be
typed directly after the relevant text [3] or in separate

[3] If footnotes are typed within the text, be sure to indent
or mark them in some way so they catch the copy editor's
eye and she can style them.

lists chapter by chapter. Ask the publishers for their
preference. If you are typing scholarly work, with
footnotes, a style manual is essential. See the recommendations in Chapter 3 and Appendix II. Foreign
accent marks—tilde (ñ), umlaut (ü), cedilla (ç), cir-
cumflex (ô), grave (è) and aigue (é)—are best drawn
in by hand, unless your typewriter has these symbols.

An assignment, must be proofread before you turn
it in. The easiest way is to have someone read the
original to you while you check your typing; if a
reader is unobtainable, you will have to proofread it
yourself. Read Chapter 4 to learn how to proofread.
Be professional: If you must correct your manuscript,
use the proper marks (see pages 112–113).

The simplest way to get a proofreading assignment
might be to ask the editor or production editor, when
you bring or send in your typing, if you can proofread
the galleys later on. If you check your typing carefully, you can probably do a good job on the galleys.
It is especially interesting to see a manuscript you

have typed after others have gone over it—you can see just what an editor or copy editor does. In this way you can develop a knowledge of their work and perhaps someday decide to try your hand at it.

Typing rates in New York City average $1 a page, with extra for a carbon copy. Outside New York, rates are lower. Rates are constantly changing, however, so discover the going rate before applying for work. Check the local college paper and call any typists who advertise, to find what the average rates are where you live. Colleges are an excellent source of typing jobs— from a sophomore's term paper to a doctoral candidate's thesis to a professor's book-length manuscript. Check the sources listed in Chapter 2, to see which publishers regularly hand out typing assignments. All possible sources for editorial work mentioned in Chapter 2 can also be checked for typing jobs.

MANUSCRIPT REPORTS

In most publishing houses editorial assistants wade through the unsolicited manuscripts. But when the load becomes too great, freelancers may be called on to do first readings and rake out the absolute locoweed and poison ivy. A manuscript reader, whether in-house or freelance, is expected to file a brief appraisal, usually no more than one typed page, on a standard report form provided by the publisher. This most often asks for no more than a brief plot outline; an opinion—favorable or not—of the author's style, pacing, and development of characters; and of course anything that might be relevant to promotion and

sales. To give you an idea of what's called for, here's
a sample reader's report:

TITLE *Snobs and Supersnobs; the British Aristocrats*
RECEIVED *July 5, 1979*
AUTHOR / AGENT *Elizabeth Bennett (author) Fitzwilliam
Darcy (agent)*
FIRST READER: Please summarize plot & give positive
& negative aspects of the book, including unusual selling
points.

A humorous analysis of the English (and Anglophilic
American) upper classes, done in the tone of a sociological
manual ("Groups of up to twenty gather regularly to chase
a small reddish-brown mammal across the fields, assisted
by a pack of dogs, and themselves on horseback. Despite
the numerical and technical superiority of the men-horse-
dog side, this activity is considered a fair sport.") Various chapters deal with schools and universities, the upper
class at play (including fox-hunting, Ascot & Derby, and
adultery), the u.c. at war, the aristocracy hierarchy, etc. All
this has been done before—and better—by various Mitfords. Though the humor is labored at times, the book
has its merits. The author's own social standing (she is a
countess) cannot fail to stimulate sales.
RECOMMENDATION: *Second reading*
READER: *SKL*
DATE: *8/20/79*

SECOND READER: I found it delightful, though it could
certainly use a bit of polishing and tightening up in spots.
I agree that the Mitfords have trod the same ground, but I
think there is always room in these troubled times for a
lighthearted spoof, especially one that will sell to (1)
aristos anxious to see what a certified blueblood has said,
(2) aristophiles who will buy anything a certified blueblood

has written, & (3) aristophobes who buy anything that knocks the establishment—especially from within.
RECOMMENDATION: *Acceptance*
READER: *JA*
DATE: *9/4/79*

Manuscript readers tend to be very hard on books. Every year, the first assignment in the Radcliffe Publishing Procedures course (page 223) is to read and report on a novel, and recommend its "acceptance" or "rejection." The novel is invariably an already published classic of world literature—and just as invariably it is rejected by nine-tenths of the neophyte editors taking the course.

Besides having a broad enough background in literature to appreciate what is good and what is bad, and enough self-confidence in one's own judgment to make a firm decision, manuscript readers should keep up with publishing trends (i.e., Bicentennial in 1976; psychological self-help in 1977; jogging in 1978) so as to anticipate the market rather than glut it, and have a healthy respect for sales possibilities. Some books, especially poetry and belles lettres, are published purely for love. But if a publisher is to remain solvent—and be able to do some books purely for love —other works must be published for money.

Freelancers who would like to do manuscript reading should inquire routinely at every publishing house with which they work. Judging by the responses to our questionnaire, payment is by the manuscript rather than by the hour—so your income would depend on your reading speed.

EXPERT READERS

A new work on paleontology is generally sent to a paleontologist for appraisal before it is accepted by the publisher (preferably not an expert who has just published a book on the same subject—or is just about to). Fees for such expert reading run upward from $50. If you have expert knowledge of some field, check *LMP* for publishers whose specialties coincide with yours, and write to ask if they have any manuscripts to be evaluated. Generally, though, this work is handed out through the "old boy" circuit of university professors. An expert reader judges a book's *accuracy* and *scholarly merit;* a manuscript reader assesses *salability* and *literary merit.*

RESEARCH

Publishers hire researchers to check new editions and revise facts and statistics, particularly when the author is dead or otherwise unavailable for this task, or to check research on a nonfiction book by an author who is remote from the resources of a large-city public library. Sometimes so many months elapse between the acceptance of a manuscript and the publication of the book that the facts have to be rechecked.

Many researchers work directly for authors; New York's *Village Voice* newspaper regularly carries advertisements from authors looking for research assistance. The pay is never that good, but the hours of work are flexible, the work—one hopes—is interesting, and the experience valuable. Since researchers work directly with the author, there is a good chance your "invaluable services" will be praised in the book's acknowledgments section—a solid recommendation for future jobs.

Doing research on any topic is almost impossible without the facilities of a large public library. There are some private research libraries, such as the Athenaeum (Boston), the Morgan and the special collections of the New York Public Library (New York City), the Newbery and John Crerar (Chicago), and the Huntington (San Marino, California), open to serious researchers. In order to use these collections you must apply to the library and describe the research you intend to do. University libraries are sometimes open to the public. If you are doing freelance research for a professor, he may be able to arrange for you to use his university's collection. Other research collections have been assembled by the larger museums; naturally, these will be focused on the same field—art or natural science or history— as is the museum collection. There are still some private libraries with invaluable research material. If you were doing research for a book on John D. Rockefeller I, for example, the Rockefeller family *might* furnish some research material or recommend a research source.

On almost any subject—cooking, sewing, sports, theater—there exists an authoritative encyclopedia or dictionary or yearly record book; *Who-What-When-Where-How-Why Made Easy* by Mona McCormick lists many of these.

In the library you should investigate the card catalog (praying that it is complete and up-to-date) for books on your subject, and the *Reader's Guide to Periodic Literature* for magazine articles. Do not just accept or reject the book as a source on the basis of the catalog card; check the actual book whenever possible. This is essential when doing scholarly bibliographic research, where the difference in the wording of the title or the placement of the author's name on the title page may differ from the rare First to the common Second Edition. Such slight differences are important in bibliography and are so subtle they cannot be ascertained from the catalog cards. The cards, if typed by a careless or drowsy assistant, may even be in error. Some more tips for researchers: Do not abbreviate when copying. Later on you may want to know whether the title is *Man & Mammal* or *Man and Mammal*. Put clear, exaggerated quotation marks around quotes to distinguish from paraphrases of the text. If your writing hand holds out, copy quotations from the text in every case. You can paraphrase later but you cannot recast a paraphrase as a quotation.

Fees for researching vary—find out what the going rate is. Specialized research, especially if you qualify as an expert in the field, should pay more.

PICTURE EDITING AND PICTURE RESEARCH

The responsibilities of a picture editor may be as broad as "here is a biography of Woodrow Wilson; we need fifty to a hundred photos or prints, and the total photo budget is $3000." Or they may be as narrow as obtaining permissions for a list of already selected illustrations. There are three different aspects of photo research; freelancers can get assignments to do one, two, or all three.

FINDING THE PERFECT ILLUSTRATION

Since the invention of the camera in 1826, billions of photos have been taken. In addition to sorting through what must sometimes seem like a substantial percentage of these, a picture editor must winnow through drawings and prints, photos of works of art, photostats of historic headlines, and famous letters and documents.

In order to keep track of what photographs are available, and from whom, an aspiring or even prospering picture editor *must*, according to an experienced picture editor with over twenty years in the field, keep a detailed card file of picture sources. The file should have a record of free and for-sale picture sources and be cross-referenced to subject matter. If someday you get a rush call for an aerial view of New York City, you can check your file under "aerial shots—cities" and come up with the name(s) of the right photographer(s).

Some pictures are free and some cost money. The facts of publishing life being what they are, the enterprising picture editor will have to track down free photos—if only to have budget money left to pay for the rights to one great photo by a famous news photographer. For researchers in the New York City area, nothing beats the general reference and picture collections of the New York Public Library. Not every picture in the vast assortments is free, but many prints are out of copyright. In any case, browsing here will give you an excellent idea of the types of illustrative material available. Your best guide is another book published on the same subject. You can pick up leads to free material and to photographers from the photo credits (write to the book's publisher to get addresses). Illustrated magazines, particularly regional ones, have a wealth of photos and prints, some available for the asking. Other free picture sources include U.S. Government agencies, tourist offices of foreign governments, publicity departments of large corporations. Some formerly free photo sources—museums and galleries—are now beginning to charge fees for their pictures.

Paid-for photos come from photographers and their agents. One reason for keeping that detailed file is to have on hand a list of photographers and photo agencies, what their fees are, and notes of what types of pictures they specialize in. If you are just starting out as a picture editor, check *LMP* and the phone book for all the photo agencies in your area, write to them, and introduce yourself. If you are a total newcomer to the field, it helps to have a letter of introduction from a publisher for whom you are doing an assignment. Ask each agency for a fee schedule and a list of their specialties. Try to set up an appointment to go through their files to get an idea of what they have on hand. When their replies come in, note all the details on your index cards, but do not discard the letters (if any questions arise later about fees, you will have the facts in writing). In any letters you get from an agency, pay special attention to the fine print. Agency fee scales vary enormously, and some may be ruinously expensive if you fail to note conditions.

Agencies charge three kinds of fees. First of all, there may be a fee for you to look through their files—for photos of President Wilson, for example. If an agency staff member checks the files, you may be charged a search fee. Second, there is a holding fee for photos or transparencies in your possession and still under consideration. Usually this starts after two weeks. If you need the photos any longer, ask for an extension; holding fees are charged per photo per week, so they can mount up rapidly. Third, there is a permissions fee for the right to reproduce any photo you do select (you should not have to pay holding fees for the photos you do use; that would be paying double).

GETTING PERMISSION TO USE A PICTURE

Locating the ideal photograph is not enough. Even if you have the actual photograph in your possession, you must still get permission to reproduce it. Rights to reproduce a photo must be secured from the photographer, his agent, or heirs. You should get a signed permissions form even for free photos from tourist offices and such, in case someone changes his mind after it is too late to pull the photo from the book. If you cannot locate the photographer, send a registered letter to his last known address and offer to pay X dollars (whatever you are paying the other photographers). Quite a few publishers do not want to use photos for which they do not have written permission; in these cases the photo editor must become an amateur detective, trying to track down missing artists.

Your request for permission should specify the

rights your publisher wants: North American, world-wide in English, worldwide. The wider the market for which you seek rights, the higher the fee (if any) will tend to be. To complicate matters, if the photo is of a work of art, you must obtain the right to repro-duce the art object as well as that specific pho-tograph. Hopefully this permission may be obtained by writing to the owner of the art object, who may then refer you to someone else who owns the rights. (If the artist is alive, he or she may own the reproduc-tion rights, but not the work of art.) Check with the actual owner *first*.

If there are people in the photo, and it is not a news photo, the photographer should have gotten re-leases from the subjects, whether or not they are pro-fessional models. Just to be safe, doublecheck and make sure that he has. Otherwise, do not use it.

FINDING OUT WHAT IT IS ALL ABOUT

Once the photos have been selected and fee pay-ment arranged (fees are usually paid on the book's publication date), another researcher goes to work, assembling information about the contents of the photo so a caption can be written. When artwork is being used for an illustration, the researcher works in advance to determine (or provide information so the editor and art editor can determine) exactly what should be included in the artwork. Photographers frequently supply content information (sometimes only on repeated request), but this should be regarded with a skeptical eye. Photographers are not always experts in identification; the researcher should make sure that "*Amanita* mushroom" or "St.

Patrick's Cathedral" is really that. Like text research, this work involves long hours of slogging through encyclopedias and other reference books, old newspapers and magazines, etc.

Picture research pays about the same as other research, but picture editing can pay four or five times as much. To earn such fees you need lots of experience; to get started in the field you need an eye for a good photo and a sense of the overall design of the book. A good way to start is by taking a beginner's course in photography at an evening school or from a photographer (check with colleges, universities, and professional photographers in your area to see who might be giving such a course).

A final tip: Once you begin to work with loaned-out glossies and transparencies, get some sort of insurance to protect you in case of loss, by you or by someone else (such as an engraver or printer) while the photos are your responsibility. A lost photo, like a lost manuscript, becomes more priceless than pearls.

TRANSLATING

If you have a thorough idiomatic knowledge of English *and* of a foreign language, you can get work translating into English, from English into your other language, or copyediting or editing books published in this country in that language. Quite a bit of foreign-language publishing is done in the United States—not only textbooks but also novels, scholarly works, newspapers, and magazines. For example, Alex-

ander Solzhenitsyn's *August 1914* was published in
America in both English and Russian. Many books are
now produced with the original language on a left-hand
page and the English translation on the right (especially
poetry). Those "foreign languages" for which publishers seek translators include London cockney rhyming
slang and Australian outback dialect.

The major problem in translating is retaining fidelity to the original while achieving an idiomatic use
of English. A computer, baffled by idioms, cannot do
it. One computer, translating from English to Russian, rendered "out of sight, out of mind" as "invisi-
ble and insane." But an ingenious translator may be
able to come up with an idiom of equivalent meaning. Puns and allusions are also challenges. One reason poetry is most difficult to translate is that besides
contending with meter and rhyme, the translator
must deal with the most allusive kind of language.
The publisher may have a decided preference for a
literal word-by-word translation of the original, or for
a looser translation that conveys the original *feeling*
of the book. Query before you begin work.

Translating usually pays by the word. The more ex-
otic the language and the more convoluted the original
writing, the higher the fee. Copyediting rates for foreign languages run double those for English, even for
a language as well known in this country as French. The
more obscure the language, the higher the rate you can
probably bargain for (but probably also the less demand
for your services). Linguists may also pick up assignments to do reader's reports of foreign-language books.
(See the discussion of reader's reports on page 172.)

REWRITING, EDITING, AND WRITING

If you are copyediting a book and find yourself making extensive changes (with the publisher's permission, of course) so that the text will make sense, you are no longer copyediting. Instead, you are rewriting or editing, and you *should be paid a higher rate*. Sometimes the ideas in a book are expressed clearly but in illogical sequence, and you must rearrange them. Sometimes an author knows what she wants to say (and, after several readings, you do too), but she has not managed to express herself clearly. This problem is especially likely to occur if the author's native language is not English (although, sad to say, it often happens that the imprecise English *is* her native tongue). Or her use of the language may be academic rather than colloquial. One sign of this is a subtle misuse of a common idiom: "the hair of the hound," rather than the correct "the hair of the dog." A book for a general audience authored by a scholar may be sent to a rewriter to add salt and pepper to the bland academic prose.

Rewriting pays from about the same as copyediting to twice or three times as much. Check on the going rate in your area. If you can get a steady supply of work, you may do far better financially as a freelance editor and rewriter than as an in-house editor, even considering the fringe benefits of a salaried job.

We have made no attempt in this book to cover the markets for and special problems of freelance writers, by which we mean writers who produce whole books or articles and generally choose the subjects on which they write. Certain odd bits of writing are parceled out to freelancers, including writing captions, jacket flaps, sections of books. Odd-bit writers, like chameleons, must adapt their style (or camouflage it) to suit their surroundings. If you have the capacity for this versatility (some very good writers do not—or will not alter their styles even if they can), opportunities for such work exist.

Caption or legend writing, like translating, tends to be paid by the word. A caption writer generally gets a research folder, copies of the glossies or transparencies, and specifications as to the number of characters per line and the number of lines allotted for each caption. Jacket flap writers should ideally get a copy of the manuscript or galleys; more often they receive a copy of the reader's report and a publicity department questionnaire that the author has filled out. The current fee for writing a jacket flap is $150 to $200; at that rate, it is not too hard to feign enthusiasm for the book! Straight writing, filling in odd bits of a book (usually one that is assembled by the publisher rather than written by an author) pays from $8 an hour up.

If you are interested in doing any of these writing jobs, query your regular list of publishers. The catch is that you have to have experience before you can get a job to gain experience. Dredge up some college newspaper writing out of your past, or offer to do the first assignment on spec—and get paid only if the publisher approves it. It is worth the time and the effort to be able to provide as many freelance services as possible.

Chapter 7

$, $, $ — TAXES, TAXES, TAXES

FREELANCING may not be a nine-to-five routine but it *is* a business. You'll spare yourself a lot of agonizing, and possibly some real trouble with the Internal Revenue Service, if you follow a few simple rules to put your freelancing on a businesslike basis. Keeping records of what you receive and spend is essential.

BILLING

To keep accurate records of your income, make carbon copies of all your bills—which of course should be typed. The bill (Figure 1) should include the date, the name of the person to whom it is addressed, your name and address (some publishers ask for your Social Security number as well), the name of the job, and the amount charged. You should personally sign every bill. You may submit your bill on your letterhead or on plain paper; do not bother having special invoice forms printed. On some jobs, particularly proofreading or indexing, when you may receive galleys and not the original manuscript, the material may not include the author's full name or the com-

December 5, 1979

TO: Able Press
             1776 Madison Avenue
             New York, N.Y. 10099

FROM: Susan Laurens
             2080 Madison Avenue
             New York, N.Y. 10037

             (123-45-6789)

FOR: Indexing James F. Cooper's OUR DEBT TO THE IROQUOIS

             51 hours (at $5 per hour)

             $255

Susan Laurens

Figure 1.

plete book title. Make a point of asking the publisher
for this information. You should know what you are
working on—anyway, you should be curious. Direct
your bill to a specific individual at the publisher's,
usually the person who gave you the work. It is less
likely to get lost that way. It should be labeled—
conspicuously—as a bill so that it does not get used
as a coffee cup coaster! As to how much to charge, see
Chapter 2, pages 26–28, and the chapters detailing
specific freelancing areas.

Some freelancers' records consist solely of their
copies of bills, sorted according to date billed or
sorted by publishers, and checked off in some way as
they are paid. Then, by going back over the previous
month's bills, they know whom to ask about delayed
payments. Some publishers pay within two weeks;
others, particularly smaller firms whose billing is not
automated, may let things go. You have a legitimate

reason to call or write if you have not received your
money within a month of billing, perhaps within five
or six weeks if you are not in the same city or state as
the publisher.

"Publisher's procrastination," a malady well-
known to freelancers, was deplored by many of this
book's survey respondents. A delay in paying bills by
one large publisher led some freelancers to work
only in return for payment on delivery, because previous bills had not been paid for four months.

INCOME RECORDS

Go one step further than saving your bills: Keep a
record book with a month-to-month list. A loose-leaf
notebook is adequate, although you might want to get
one of the preprinted bookkeeping records from an
office supply firm.

In the notebook keep your list of jobs and your list
of expenses for each month on facing pages. Include
the date you submitted the bill, to whom billed and
for what job, and the amount billed. It is also sometimes helpful to jot down the number of pages or
galleys in the assignment for your own information.
Leave a space to note the day you get paid. Once you
have organized your records of income, it takes just a
minute to write in the information when you type
up a bill.

For tax purposes, records to substantiate income
and expenses must be kept at least three years. Since
twelve loose-leaf pages and a few envelopes of bills
and receipts do not take up much space, you should
probably hold on to your records even longer, espe-

cially if your income fluctuates from year to year and you may be eligible for income averaging (page 209) some time in the future. A file folder will easily hold all your records and your copies of income tax returns for any one year.

The main reason for keeping records, of course, is to make filing your taxes as simple a chore as possible. Figure 2, page 210, shows a typical record book. Keeping records also helps you compare your earnings from year to year, and see which are your best— and promptest-to-pay—accounts.

EXPENSE RECORDS

You should also keep a record of business expenses as they *occur*. If you put off recording your expenses you may forget what you spent or lose the receipt (hold on to receipts, if you get them, even after you record the expense). Also, it is not too bothersome to note an item or two every day, but you will have an unpleasant chore if you let things slide till the end of the month—or until tax time. This simple method of keeping records, entering expenses as they occur and income as it is received, is the *cash receipts* method of bookkeeping—the most practical for freelancers (see Figure 3, page 211, for an example). There are other bookkeeping systems, such as accrual, but in the following discussion it is assumed you will use the cash receipts method.

What are business expenses? Anything you spend to operate your business as a freelancer: materials and supplies, depreciation of furniture and equipment, rent, sales tax on purchases, repairs, insurance, transportation, advertising . . . Let's deal with them one at a time.

MATERIALS AND SUPPLIES

These include pencils, typing and carbon paper, index cards, postage, and other such paraphernalia related to your business. More permanent items, such as a typewriter, copying machine, desk, or file cabinet, are capital expenses and must be depreciated; they cannot be deducted as a lump-sum expense the year you buy them.

Reference books you need for your work, especially those with a short useful life—such as almanacs—are fully deductible in the year of purchase. According to IRS rules, reference books (such as dictionaries) with a useful life longer than one year must be depreciated rather than deducted. But unless such expenses are unusually heavy—if you buy the *Oxford English Dictionary* or *Encyclopaedia Britannica*—you can probably deduct them the year you buy them.

Newspapers and magazines are generally not deductible. You may feel it incumbent upon yourself, as a well-informed freelancer, to read *The New York Times* daily, but do not try to deduct it if you live in New York City! The IRS says you should not deduct a newspaper or magazine you would be reading in any case. You *may* deduct the cost of trade magazines such as *Publishers Weekly* or *Freelancer's Newsletter*. If you are doing research, for example, on the drug problem in major U.S. and foreign cities, and you subscribe to—or buy on a newsstand—the daily papers from these cities to obtain local coverage of the problem, that expense is deductible. If you are copyediting or indexing a book on astrology and you buy a book or magazine or two on the subject to get some background, that is deductible. Such expenses are deductible only if you buy the books or periodicals for a business purpose. Be prepared to justify your deductions.

DEPRECIATION

Major capital expenses, such as office furniture and equipment, cannot be deducted in a lump sum in the year of purchase. They must be depreciated over the useful life of the item. If your new $200 desk has a theoretical useful life of ten years, you would deduct 1/10 of the cost ($20) every year for ten years, using the straight-line method of depreciation. (It is assumed in the following discussion that you would use straight-line accounting, the least complicated method of figuring depreciation, rather than such techniques as declining balance.)

In calculating depreciation you must take into account possible salvage value: If it will be more than 10 percent of the original cost, you must subtract the salvage-value amount *over* 10 percent from your depreciation deduction. For example, if you estimate that your $200 desk will have a salvage value of $30 after ten years, you then subtract $10 ($30 minus $20—10 percent of cost) from your first year's depreciation. Thus your first year's depreciation would be $10; subsequent years, $20. The salvage-value-minus-10-percent-of-cost figure must be subtracted from your *first year's* depreciation. Do *not* attempt to spread the salvage value subtraction over the depreciation period. (That is, you should *not* subtract salvage value ($30) from cost ($200) and then take $17 depreciation yearly for ten years. You would penalize yourself and wind up with $170 total deduction instead of $190.)

If you estimate that any possible salvage value will be less than 10 percent of the original cost, you can simply ignore it in your calculations. It is up to the taxpayer—*you*—to decide what the possible salvage value will be.

What if you have been deducting 1/10 of the cost of an item every year and in the fourth year it falls apart? Simply deduct the balance of the original cost that year. For example, if your $150 typewriter goes completely haywire after four years, and so far you have deducted $45 ($15, or 1/10 of the value, yearly for three years), you would deduct the remaining $105 that fourth year. So even if you overestimate the useful life of a piece of equipment, you will get your full depreciation deduction.

What happens if you are still using something after you have depreciated the full value? You just keep on using it (of course, you do not depreciate it any more); you are not *forced* to get rid of something once it is fully depreciated. The IRS guidelines are just generalized judgments. If you feel *your* typewriter will last only five years, you may deduct 1/5 of the value annually for five years. In every case, with every item, you must make a personal judgment as to how long something is going to be useful, based on your own experience and the normal life expectancy of the item.

Used items are depreciated like new ones, except the useful life may be even shorter. Personal property converted to business use is treated like a used item. For example, you may have a three-year-old typewriter when you begin to freelance full-time. You start depreciating this on the basis of its fair market value. To determine fair market value, find out what it would cost to buy a comparable used typewriter and compare this amount with what the machine cost at the time you bought it. If you paid $150 for the machine three years ago, and the current market value of a three-year-old typewriter, same make and model, is $100, start your business depreciation at $100. This may seem quite obvious, but it is rather tricky.

Some things (houses, antique furniture) do go *up* in value over the years. If your Chippendale desk cost $500 ten years ago, and the market value is now $1000, you must start your business depreciation with the *lower* value, $500. *You always start depreciating with the lower value.* If property is used for both business and personal activities, you can deduct only the depreciation due to business use—you will have to make a reasonable estimate as to percentages of use. You should recalculate these percentages every year. If you use your $150 typewriter half the time for typing indexes and half the time for personal correspondence, your yearly depreciation deduction—assuming a useful life of ten years—would be $7.50 (1/2 of 1/10 of $150).

To depreciate any expense you *must keep records* of what you bought, when, how much you paid, and how much you have depreciated in previous years' tax returns. This is an excellent reason to hold on to your receipts and keep records.

RENT

A freelancer who rents an apartment in which she lives and also works can deduct the cost of her office space *providing* (1) the office is used exclusively for business and (2) it is used on a regular basis. The first proviso, which came in with the 1977 tax law changes, is the vital one for editorial freelancers. It mandates that you must have a specific section of your home as your principal place of business. Previously, a room could serve a dual purpose (such as bedroom and office) and the percentage attributable to work could be deducted as a business expense. As of 1977, however, a specific section of your apartment must be used as an office in order to qualify as a business expense. For example, if by judicious use of bookcases, screens, and collapsible walls you section off a portion of your apartment and use that space *only* for your work, you may safely deduct the appropriate percentage of your rent from your freelance income. (This has the added advantage of forcing you, and your friends and family, to take your work seriously.)

In figuring the deduction, you can either divide by the number of rooms or by area. Thus you would deduct one third if the office is one of three rooms—not counting bath or kitchen—in your apartment.

If you are married, and only one of you works at home as a freelancer, you would still deduct as above, if you file a joint return. If you and your spouse file separate returns, you must calculate your business rent deduction on the basis of your share of the rent, not the total rent. This also applies if you share your apartment with a roommate.

By the way, do not deduct a percentage of your

deposit (if your landlord requires one) unless you want the trouble of *adding* it the year you leave the apartment and get the deposit back.

If you own a home rather than rent, the situation becomes more complicated. As a homeowner you will be deducting your mortgage *interest* payments elsewhere in your return; as a freelancer you can deduct a percentage (1) of your mortgage equity (principal) payments, (2) of your property taxes, and (3) of the depreciation on your *house. You may not take "depreciation" of the cost of the land.* All three of these deductions must take into account the percentage of floor space in your house devoted to business use. In deducting for equity payment, you must know how much of your mortgage payment is for interest charges and how much for principal; your mortgage should list, for each year's payments, the percentage applied to interest and the percentage applied to principal. In deducting for property taxes, you must know how much of the tax assessment is based on the value of your house, and how much—if any—on the land. Your depreciation deduction must take into account the useful life of your house— which may be as long as fifty years—and the original cost of the *house.* Using one of the six rooms in your $30,000 house as an office, you could take a yearly depreciation of $100 (1/6 × 1/50 × $30,000). If taxes on your house came to $600 a year, you could deduct 1/6, or $100; and if your mortgage equity payment for the year was $900, you could deduct 1/6, or $150.

According to some tax experts, it might be possible to set an arbitrary figure as office "rent" (what you would pay to rent an office comparable to the one in your home) and deduct that instead of having to calculate all these percentages. Ask your own tax expert—or the IRS—about the feasibility of this. If you sell your house, your tax return for the year of sale will have to take into account any profit or loss on the sale. At this point you should consult an expert—if you have not done so already! Ask your accountant, lawyer, or the IRS for advice.

SALES TAX

The sales tax on business purchases is fully deductible. The simplest way to handle this deduction is to include the tax with the price when you record your purchases.

REPAIRS

Fixing your typewriter or painting your office is a business expense and may be deducted. If you as a homeowner must repair a leaky roof, you are entitled to deduct a percentage of the cost (the same percentage as office space/total area) if the repair does not add value or useful life to your house, but only restores the status quo.

INSURANCE

If you have insurance against fire, theft, and personal liability—assuming you do not live in a city where it is virtually impossible to get any insurance, except for the Federal Crime Insurance available through insurance agents—again you can deduct the percentage applicable for business. Of course, if your insurance policy covers only your typewriter and copying machine, you would be entitled to deduct the entire cost. You might investigate *valuable*

papers insurance, which will at least partially repay
you if anything happens to your files, research notes,
or irreplaceable material from a publisher.

OTHER OFFICE EXPENSES

Just as you deduct a percentage of your rent, you
may deduct a comparable percentage of your electricity and heating fuel bills. If you feel justified in deducting a higher percentage (for example, if you have
an electric typewriter or would not be home during
the day with the lights turned on if you were not
freelancing), be prepared to prove it—perhaps by
showing how your electric bill jumped sharply the
month you began to work at home.

You may also deduct the percentage of your telephone bill applicable to business, and the percentage
of your answering service—if you have one—used for
business. There is no hard-and-fast rule for such deductions; you must make a fair and reasonable estimate of the business/personal percentages. If you
do a lot of business telephoning, you might consider
having a separate phone installed. Then you could
deduct all of the phone bill as a business expense, as
well as all of the cost, if any, of the answering service
or phone-answering device.

TRANSPORTATION

A salaried employee cannot deduct, as a business
expense, the money spent getting to and from the
place of business. However, as a freelancer your
home is your place of business, so you may deduct
your expenses in picking up and delivering assignments. You may decide whether to use a bus, train,

taxicab, your own car, or a messenger service. You need not get receipts for bus, train, or cab fares; just keep a record of how much you spend each month. However, this pick-up and delivery expense must be "ordinary and necessary"; if you claim $5 in cab fares for each job, even those paying only $20, the deduction might well be questioned—unless, of course, you can reach the publisher only by cab, and $5 is the standard fare.

If you use your automobile to pick up and deliver work, or to drive to and from the Post Office to mail it in, you may deduct the operating expenses. Keep a record of your actual expenses—gas, oil, toll and parking fees—while using the car for business. Deduct these expenses outright, as well as the applicable percentage of total depreciation, repairs, and insurance. Or keep a record of your business mileage and apply the IRS formula. (The exact allowances can vary from year to year, so consult the IRS publication on *Travel, Entertainment and Gift Expenses* before computing your deduction). This per-mile deduction includes gas, oil, insurance, depreciation, and repairs, but you may still deduct toll and parking lot fees in addition.

If your assignment necessitates a trip to the library or elsewhere to do some research, you may also deduct the cost of that trip.

A part-time freelancer who has a salaried job as well may deduct travel expenses only from her place of business to where she picks up and delivers her freelance assignment. (Read that again. It is important.) A part-time freelancer who commutes daily from Connecticut to a job in midtown Manhattan may *not* deduct her commutation expense on those days she also goes downtown to pick up a freelance assignment. The only allowable deduction would be the cost of bus or cab fare between her midtown office and the publisher's office, and back.

If you move your place of residence, and thus also your place of business, you may deduct as a business expense that percentage of the mover's bill applicable to moving your office furniture and equipment, supplies, files, and reference books.

ADVERTISING AND PROMOTION

You may deduct the cost of advertising your availability for freelance work, including sending solicitations to various publishers. You may also deduct the cost of sending Christmas cards to publishers or entertaining editors in the expectation of getting work. If you entertain editors for whom you do work, or for whom you would like to—and conceivably could—work, the expense, whether at your home or elsewhere, is deductible. You may deduct the cost of a party, even if not all the guests are business associates, if you can show that you had it purely for business; that you would not have had it if not in the expectation of getting more business. You need not discuss business matters at the party, and you need not prove that you did get some assignments as a result of the party, *but your intent must be purely to get more business.*

It is important for entertainment expenses to keep precise records of the date of the party (or restaurant lunch date or whatever), who was invited, their business connection with you, and food and liquor expenses. You *must* save receipts for expenses over $25 (it is a good idea to save any bills for party expenses).

CHILD CARE

The cost of having someone care for your child, your mentally or physically disabled spouse, or an incapacitated dependent is deductible—even if you work at home and even if only part-time—if you can show that without paid help you would be unable to work. The cost is converted into a tax credit amounting to 20 percent of up to $2000 in care expenses for one dependent, and up to $4000 for two or more dependents. Thus the maximum credit is $400 for one and $800 for two or more. This credit is not tied into an earnings ceiling. Low earnings can have an effect, however: If you incur expenses of $4000 for care of two dependents but you earned only $3000, your credit would be 20 percent of your earnings ($600 rather than $800).

The credit is subtracted from the amount of tax you owe. It is entered on Schedule A, not as a business deduction.

Outside child care for dependents under the age of fifteen, as in a day-care center, nursery school, or baby-sitter's home, is also deductible. Costs are treated as for care inside your home (see above).

Another expense qualifying for the credit is the cost of ordinary domestic service such as laundry, cleaning, or cooking (but not payments to a gardener or to a chauffeur).

If your paid help is a relative, seek advice from an IRS

expert as to whether you can claim the credit.

EDUCATION

The IRS policy on education expenses all but rules out deductions by freelancers. For course fees to be deducted, the course must be taken to *maintain a skill* required for your present work, *not* to get a new job. Therefore the only possible deductible courses would seem to be those in copyediting or proofreading skills. And even these are deductible only if essential to maintain your skills; not, for example, to become a copy editor if you now only proofread.

BAD DEBTS

These are deductible the year the debt becomes worthless, not necessarily the year the debt occurs. (For example, if the publisher who has owed you money since 1978 goes bankrupt in 1980, you can deduct on 1980 taxes.) You can deduct as a bad debt only the expenses you incurred (cost of materials, transportation), *not your own services*, as on your original bill. However, if you entered and reported this amount as income, even though you received nothing, you may later deduct it all as a bad debt. This complication is another good argument for using cash receipts accounting, listing as income only what you have actually received.

Similarly, if you submit a bill for $100 and receive only $50, you cannot deduct $50 as a bad debt. Your only recourse in such a case would be to sue—and it would undoubtedly cost far more than $50 just to go to court. Just do not ever do another job for anyone who has stung you once. Maybe not even if he finally pays up and apologizes. There are enough honest, aboveboard publishers that you need not deal with the occasional oddball.

SUBCONTRACTING

If you hire another freelancer as a typist or researcher, the fee paid is a business expense. But be careful as to the conditions you set down. If you specify where or when the work is to be done—for example, in your office between 9 A.M. and 5 P.M.—you have entered into an employer–employee relationship and are liable for withholding, disability, and Social Security payments. You may set a deadline and specify style requirements, just as a publisher gives you a style sheet for copyediting or a character-per-line and line count for indexing. If your hired freelancer has to account to you only as to the finished project on a predetermined date, then she or he is an independent subcontractor and your responsiblity is no more than any publisher's responsibility to you as a freelancer.

You should, however, keep track of how much money you pay to other freelancers who do work for you as independent contractors. You must file a form with the IRS for any independent contractor to whom you pay more than $600. A copy of the form should go to that person. In addition, you must file a summary form. So if Jack Jefferson did $715 of typing for you, and Milly Peters did $650 of research, you would file a form for each of them and a form summarizing both payments. You may need an Employer Identification Number—check with IRS.

OTHER DEDUCTIONS

If you get a freelance job through an agent or an employment agency, you may deduct the fee you paid. If your maid cleans your office, you may deduct for that portion of time she spends on it. If you use a messenger service, instead of making pickups and deliveries yourself, you may deduct the costs. The cost of duplicating or Xeroxing work before you send it out (almost essential if you are mailing the work to a publisher in another city) is deductible. Dues to professional organizations (such as the American Society of Indexers or writers' clubs) and fees paid to attend seminars or meetings of such professional groups are also deductible. If you give your messenger service a generous tip you can deduct up to $25 as a business expense.

ESTIMATED TAX

According to law, if you expect to owe $100 or more in federal tax you must file an estimated tax declaration, Form 1040-ES. This consists of four declaration-vouchers; you pay estimated tax four times a year as employees pay withholding tax each payday.

If you are an employee and also freelance, you might choose to take fewer exemptions on your salary withholding so that you will not have to bother with the estimated tax. Similarly, if your husband is an employee and you file a joint return, he can increase his withholding payments to cover your freelance income.

Unlike regular income tax forms, filed the year *after* you earn the income, estimated tax is due on or before April 15, June 15, September 15, and January 15 of the year in which you earn the income. How do you estimate future income? The first payment is due April 15. By April 1 your records will show your earnings for January through March. Just multiply by four to arrive at an estimate. Or you may base your estimate on your previous year's income.

As the year passes, keep a running total of your income. If you find that you are earning a great deal more or less than your original estimate, revise subsequent payments up or down. By January 15 following the tax year, you should have paid in at least *80 percent* of your actual tax (which will be determined later, when you file your return). If you have not paid in enough, you may be subject to penalty charges.

In states and cities that impose income taxes, you may have to file estimates and make quarterly payments for these as well.

By keeping a running tally of your income you will have a good idea of what your taxes will be. Actually, paying quarterly is a lot less painful than having to come up with the whole year's taxes at once.

For more details about filing estimated tax, ask the IRS for their publication on *Tax Withholding and Declaration of Estimated Tax.*

YOUR TAX RETURN

Of course in addition to filing estimated tax you

must still file a regular income tax form before April
15 of the following year. As a freelancer you will
need to file forms in addition to the basic form. These
are Schedule C, *Profit (or Loss) from Business or Profession,* and Schedule SE, *Computation of Social Security
Self-Employment Tax.* If you have kept accurate records throughout the year, you should not have too
much trouble filling them out. When you do your taxes
you will find that you are not required to supply as
many details as should be in your records. However, if
you are called in to explain expenses or deductions, you
must produce evidence as to the validity of what you
have claimed.

SCHEDULE C

This should include all your business income and
expenses. Income, incidentally, should be considered earned in the year you receive it, not the year
you submit the bill. However, do not try asking for
delayed payments from June to January to keep
down a particular year's income. You may, though,
submit an assignment January 2 rather than December 31.

It is not true, by the way, that *all* freelancers' returns are audited. The computers that handle every
return are programmed to sort out the "suspicious"
returns as well as those with errors in arithmetic or
entering (get a good pocket calculator; see Appendix
II). But if you claim 60 percent of your gross income as
business expenses. . . . Of course you could have legitimate expenses that high, but it is so unlikely you had
better be prepared to document the claim.

SOCIAL SECURITY

Self-employed persons must pay their own self-employment tax (which is the same as Social Security tax). The computation is fairly straightforward once you have completed your business income and expenses form. You must have a Social Security account number if you are subject to self-employment tax; apply for it on an appropriate form at a Social Security or IRS office. In figuring your Social Security, "you must claim all allowable deductions. You may not increase your Social Security coverage and ultimate benefits by failing to deduct all allowable items, including depreciation" (IRS Publication, *Information on Self-Employment Tax*).

Self-employment tax payments are included in the installment payments of estimated income tax paid quarterly (see pages 203–204).

If you become disabled and cannot work, you may be eligible for Social Security benefits if you have earned enough credit. Any Social Security office can give you the details.

"MISCELLANEOUS INCOME" FORM

Many publishers ask you to supply your Social Security number on your bills. They need this information when filing a form declaring "miscellaneous income" with IRS, which they are required to do if they pay you more than $600 in a calendar year. You should receive a carbon copy of the form; check the total right away. If there is a discrepancy between your records and what the publisher's form states, get in touch with the publisher at once. It is your responsibility to resolve any discrepancy with the publisher and see that a revised form is sent to IRS.

You should receive a carbon of every form from every publisher for whom you did more than $600 of work during the year. But do not assume that because you have not received a carbon IRS has not received an original!

Once you have completed Schedules C and SE, the rest of your income tax return proceeds almost as for a salaried employee.

RETIREMENT PLANS

Social Security payments are not really enough to support you once you retire. Unless you are working in an office, you are ineligible for a pension plan. Of course, not working in an office also means you will not one day automatically be considered too old to work. Eventually, though, you may want to retire, and regulations have been set up to allow deductible retirement plans for the self-employed.

The basic plan (sometimes known as the Keogh plan) lets a self-employed person invest up to 15 percent of net income each year or $7500, whichever is less, with a bank, insurance company, mutual fund, or similar institution. If your self-employed income is $750 to $5000 and your adjusted gross is $15,000 or less, you may invest up to $750 even though this is more than 15 percent of earned income. Deductible contributions can be made at any time up to the due date of your return. All of this is deductible from gross income to

arrive at adjusted gross income. So in addition to putting some money into an interest-bearing savings plan,
you are lowering your gross income and therefore your
tax. Note, however, that if your income is low you may
not get any real tax advantage. When you begin drawing on this money after retirement, you will have to pay
income tax on it, but presumably you will then be in a
much lower tax bracket.

Even if you become a salaried employee at some
point, the money you have already invested continues
to earn interest. If you do some freelancing in addition
to your salaried job, you can continue the Keogh plan.

You may not receive benefits from the plan before you
reach age 59½, unless you are totally disabled before
then. In case of a dire emergency you can withdraw the
money, but you will have to pay taxes and may have to
pay a penalty besides.

IRS Publications on *Retirement Plans for Self-
Employed Individuals* and *Questions and Answers on
Retirement Plans for the Self-Employed* give more details. Those banks, insurance companies, and stock
brokers that administer such plans also have brochures
available.

INCOME AVERAGING

This is designed for people whose incomes fluctu-
ate, such as freelancers, but is more applicable to
freelance writers who get royalties than to editorial
workers who, being paid by the hour, have earning
power limited by their physical and mental capacity,
rather than by the vagaries of book sales.

But if your several lean years have been followed by a fat one, you may be able to save some tax money. Income averaging allows you to pay some of your tax at a lower rate; the less you have earned in the preceding four years, the lower that rate will be. In order to make use of income averaging, you must have been a U.S. citizen or resident for the entire five-year period, you must have been furnishing at least half of your own support, and your income in the fifth (fat) year must exceed by more than $3000 an amount that is 20 percent greater than the average of your taxable income in the four preceding years. Unless there is quite a jump in your income, you will not save more than a few dollars. Incidentally, the rule about furnishing half of your own support means that most new college graduates cannot income average their first year's income after graduation! The IRS can supply you with publications that will explain all the conditions.

MEDICAL INSURANCE

Most freelancers have no medical insurance—a dangerous financial risk in this day and age. If you are employed before becoming a full-time freelancer, *convert your group policy to an individual payment plan*, no matter how healthy you feel. It will be more expensive and pay less benefits than a group plan, but it is a lot better than nothing. If you have not had a group policy, you may be able to obtain Blue Cross/Blue Shield or another kind of health insurance on an individual basis.

December 1979 Income

Date Billed	To Whom, For What	Amt. Billed		Date Pd.
Dec. 5	Able Press: index, James F. Cooper			
	OUR DEBT TO THE IROQUOIS	$255	00	Dec. 22
Dec. 12	Ency. Knickerbocker: proofread,			
	J.K., "Sanitation in New York"	$23	50	Dec. 19
Dec. 18	Baker Books: index, A. Lee Baba,			
	CRIMINAL SOCIETY IN IRAQ	$278	00	Dec. 29
Dec. 24	Carter Publ.: proofread, Crime			
	Classics, Dickens, OLIVER TWIST	$35	00	Jan. 20
Dec. 28	Dillard Publ.: copyedit, U.S. Grant,			
	ALCOHOL & EFFICIENCY IN			
	MODERN BUSINESS	$221	00	Jan. 5
	Total for month $556 50			
	Total for year to date $9275.80			

[1] Using the simplest, most common bookkeeping system, cash accrual, income is considered earned in the year it is received. The Carter and Dillard assignments should be reentered in the January 1974 records, and reported to the IRS as 1974 income.

Figure 2.

December 1979 Expenses

	This Month	Basis	Year to Date	
Rent	$50.00	⅓ of $150 rent, 1 room of 3	$600	00
Electricity	$8.15	⅓ of total	$53	75
Telephone	$3.54	½ of total	$42	50
Repairs	$13.50	Repainting office, December 5 (Macy's paint dept.)	$13	50
Office Supplies	$10.50	Goldsmith's $5.50 " $5.00	$157	85
Postage	$2.00		$25	30
Transportation	$20.00	Ten round trips home to Holbr. to pick up and deliver work	$350	00
Promotion	$53.00	$43 dinner 12/15/73 for eds. from Baker, Dillard, Carter. $10 12/20/73 for ad in PW.	$273	00
Subcontracts	$25.00	Betty Reader for typing Baba & Cooper indexes, 12/17/73	$210	00
Capital Expenses (Depreciation)		Furn. (desk & file)	$250	00
		Equip. (typewriter)	$150	00

Dinner 12/15/73
  Betty Johnson (Carter Pbl.)
  George Miller (Baker Bks.)
  David Scott (Baker Bks.)
  Nancy Smythe (Dillard)

Figure 3.

Appendix I

TECHNICAL TERMS

AA: Author's alteration

Alternate spellings: two equally correct and accepted ways to spell the same word—"ax" or "axe"

Ampersand: the name for the symbol "&"

Artwork: illustrative material

Back matter: everything after the last text page (appendixes, glossaries, bibliography, index); also called end matter

Blues: final proofs before a book is offset-printed

Boldface (noun and verb): **boldface** type; to mark or set something in **boldface** type

Bullets: large, boldface dots

Caps: CAPITAL letters

Caption: identifying heading *above* table, text, photograph, or art

Clear for 10: to indent the first nine numbers in a list so they will align with the following two-digit numbers

Compositor: typesetter

Copy (noun): manuscript

Cuts: engravings; all illustrative material for letterpress printing

Em dash: a dash as wide as the letter m in the type being used

En dash: a dash as wide as the letter n in the type being used (half as wide as an em dash); most frequently used in place of the word "to"

End matter: *see* Back matter

Extract (noun): long quotation set off from main text by smaller type, by narrower measure, or by space above and below (or a combination of these techniques)

Face: any style of type

Figure: numeral; illustration

Flush left/right: type set to the extreme left/right margin

Folio: page number

Font: all the type (letters and signs) in one size of one type face

Front matter: everything before page one (title page, foreward, acknowledgments, dedication, contents page); front matter is usually numbered with lowercase roman numerals

Galley or galley proof: long sheets of cheap paper on which the type is first printed, unpaged

Hanging indent: line not set to full measure but indented on the left-hand side (often used for lines following the first line in a list, with the first line set to full measure—entries in this appendix are examples)

Head: type set apart from main text to describe what follows, such as chapter head, subhead, running head

House: publishing company

Itals: *italic* type

Jacket: paper cover on a hard-cover book

Justify (verb): to set a line of type to a specified width

Kill: to delete

Leaders: series of dots "leading" the reader's eyes along a line from one word to another; often used in tables

Leading: space between letters or lines of type; or the thin metal strips used to make the spaces

Legend: identifying words *below* table, photograph, or art

Letterspace: to put e x t r a s p a c e between letters

List (noun): titles of books published by a particular house, as "the spring list"

Lowercase: uncapitalized letters

Measure (noun): width of a full line of type

Mechanicals: Pasted-down corrected proofs, plus artwork, ready to be photographed for offset printing

Middle matter: text
Parens: parentheses
PE: printer's error
Point: measure of type height, approximately 1/72 inch
Proof (noun): paginated reproduction of type before the final printing
Ragged right: unaligned right-hand margin
Roman type: ordinary type, as opposed to *italics*
Rule: line
Run in (verb): to merge a paragraph with the preceding or following one
Running foot: words at the bottom of a page accompanying the folio
Running head: words at the top of a page accompanying the folio
Signature: pages of a book printed on one sheet of paper (usually sixteen pages); every book is divided into signatures for printing
Slug (noun): full line of type
Slug (verb): to check page proofs against galleys by comparing each line of type
Small caps: SMALL CAPITAL LETTERS
Stet: literally, "let it stand"; an instruction to ignore any markings or changes and to keep original wording
Style sheet: list of style alternatives for a specific manuscript
Subscript: type set lower than normal: vitamin B_2
Superscript: type set higher than normal: $a^2+b^2=c^2$
Title(s): book(s)
Trade books: general fiction and nonfiction (as opposed to textbooks and reference works)
Underscore: underline
Uppercase: CAPITAL letters
Variant spelling: a secondary way to spell a word, usually less accepted—"wooly" is the variant of "woolly"
Widow: a short line ending a paragraph at the top of a page; infrequently, a short line at the end of any paragraph

Appendix II

BOOKS, PERIODICALS, AND SUPPLIES

Following is a selected list of books, periodicals, and supplies of particular value and/or interest to freelancers.

BOOKS

DICTIONARIES

The American Heritage Dictionary of the English Language: American Heritage, New York

Concise Oxford Dictionary: Oxford University Press, New York (based on the classic—and very expensive—*Oxford English Dictionary*)

Funk & Wagnalls Standard College Dictionary: Funk & Wagnalls, c/o Thomas Y. Crowell, New York

The Random House Dictionary of the English Language (unabridged and abridged): Random House, New York

The Reader's Digest Great Encyclopedic Dictionary: Reader's Digest Association, Pleasantville, N.Y.

Webster's New World Dictionary of the American Language (2nd College Edition): World Publishing Co., Cleveland and New York (this is not THE Webster's)

Webster's Seventh New Collegiate Dictionary: G. & C. Merriam, Springfield, Mass. (the abridged version of Webster's Third, an absolute must for all freelancers)

216

Webster's Third New International Dictionary (unabridged): G. & C. Merriam, Springfield, Mass.

It is very helpful to have an unabridged dictionary, for it will include short foreign-language dictionaries and an atlas section. The premiere foreign-language dictionaries are Cassell's separate volumes on Dutch, French, German, Italian, New Latin, and Spanish, published by Funk & Wagnalls, c/o Thomas Y. Crowell, New York. Also valuable are: *Concise Dictionary of 26 Languages*, Signet Reference Books, New American Library, New York, and *International Dictionary in 21 Languages*, Philosophical Library, New York.

GRAMMAR AND USAGE

Commonsense Grammar and Style, Robert E. Morsberger: Thomas Y. Crowell, New York, 1972

A Dictionary of American-English Usage, Margaret Nicholson: Oxford University Press, New York, 1957 (based on Fowler's *Modern English Usage*)

A Dictionary of Contemporary American Usage, Bergen Evans and Cornelia Evans: Random House, New York, 1967

A Dictionary of Modern English Usage, 2nd ed., H. W. Fowler, revised and edited by Sir Ernest Gowers: Oxford University Press, New York, 1965

The Elements of Style, William Strunk, Jr., and E. B. White: Macmillan, New York, 1972 (a classic)

Harper's English Grammar, John B. Opdycke, revised and edited by Stewart Benedict: Harper & Row, New York, 1966

Modern American Usage—A Guide, Wilson Follett, edited and completed by Jacques Barzun: Hill & Wang, New York, 1966

Modern American Usage: The Consensus, Roy Copperud: Van Nostrand Reinhold, New York, 1970

In addition, Theodore M. Bernstein, long associated with *The New York Times*, has written outstanding books on English usage—outstanding for their delightful readability as well as their information. Don't miss them! *Watch Your Language*, Channel Press, Manhasset, N.Y., 1958; *More Language That Needs Watching* (1962) and *The Careful Writer* (1965), Atheneum, New York; *Miss Thistlebottom's Hobgoblins* (1971), Farrar, Straus & Giroux, New York; *Bernstein's Reverse Dictionary* (1975), Quadrangle, New York; *Do's Don'ts, and Maybes of English Usage* (1977), Quadrangle, New York

INDEXING BOOKS

Indexing Books, Robert L. Collison: Ernest Benn Ltd., London, 1962; revised edition, John de Graff, Tuckahoe, N.Y., 1967

Indexing Your Book, Sina Spiker: University of Wisconsin Press, Madison, 1953

Training in Indexing, G. Norman Knight, ed.; M.I.T. Press, Cambridge, Mass., 1969

STYLE MANUALS

A Manual of Style, 12th ed., revised: University of Chicago Press, Chicago, 1969

Words into Type, Marjorie E. Skillin, Robert M. Gay, and others: Appleton-Century-Crofts, New York, 1974

These two books are the bibles of publishing. Other style manuals include:

American Institute of Physics, *Style Manual for Guidance in the Preparation of Papers:* New York, 1967

American Mathematical Society, "Manual for Authors of Mathematical Papers," *Bulletin of the American Mathematical Society*, vol. 68, no. 5, September 1962

American Medical Association, *Style Book — Editorial Manual:* Chicago, 1976

Conference of Biological Editors, *Style Manual for Biological Journals:* American Institute of Biological Sciences, Washington, D.C., 1964

The MLA Style Sheet, compiled by William Riley Parker: Modern Language Association of America, New York, 1970

The New York Times Manual of Style and Usage by Lewis Jordan: Times Books, New York, 1976

A Practical Style Guide for Authors and Editors, Margaret Nicholson: Holt, Rinehart and Winston, New York, 1967

United States Government Printing Office Style Manual: Government Printing Office, Washington, D.C., 1973

OTHER PARTICULARLY USEFUL REFERENCES

Bartlett's Familiar Quotations, John Bartlett, edited by Emily Morison Beck: Little, Brown, Boston, 1968

Bookmaking: The Illustrated Guide to Design and Production, Marshall Lee: Bowker, New York, 1965. The classic work on the mechanics of bookmaking

The New Columbia Encyclopedia, 4th ed., edited by William H. Harris and Judith S. Levey: Columbia University Press, New York, 1975 (a superb one-volume encyclopedia)

Concise Dictionary of American Biography: Scribner's, New York, 1964

Editors on Editing (1962) and *Publishers on Publishing* (1961), both edited by Gerald Gross: Grosset & Dunlap, New York. Fascinating anthologies by "backstage" eminences

Hammond International World Atlas, Hammond, Maplewood, N.J., 1977

The Home Book of Quotations, 10th ed., Burton Stevenson: Dodd, Mead, New York, 1967

The Home Office Guide, Leon Henry, Jr.: Home Office Press, 17 Scarsdale Farm Road, Scarsdale, N.Y. 10583

Literary Market Place (LMP): Bowker, New York; published annually

The Merriam-Webster Pocket Dictionary of Proper Names, compiled by Geoffrey Payton: Pocket Books, New York, 1972 (based on *Webster's Dictionary of Proper Names*—extremely handy, and inexpensive)

The Modern Researcher, 3rd ed., Jacques Barzun and Henry
   Graff: Harcourt, Brace, New York, 1977
"The Out-of-House Editor," *Scholarly Publishing,* April
   1972, pp. 259–272
Oxford Dictionary of Quotations: Oxford University
   Press, New York, reprinted and revised in 1970
Roget's Thesaurus, edited by Norman Lewis: G. P. Put-
   nam's, New York, 1964 (get the edition that is in alpha-
   betical order)
Webster's Biographical Dictionary: G. & C. Merriam,
   Springfield, Mass., 1976
Webster's New Geographical Dictionary: G. & C. Merriam,
   Springfield, Mass., 1977
Webster's New Dictionary of Synonyms: G. & C. Mer-
   riam, Springfield, Mass., 1968
Who-What-When-Where-How-Why Made Easy, Mona Mc-
   Cormick: Quadrangle Books, New York, 1971 (very use-
   ful guide to reference books)

PERIODICALS

Freelancer's Newsletter: P.O. Box 89, Skaneateles, New York,
   13152 (semimonthly). Freelancers may advertise their
   availability; also contains some listings from publishers, but
   leans toward freelance writers and artists
Home Office Report: Home Office Press, 17 Scarsdale
   Farm Road, Scarsdale, N.Y. 10583 (monthly). Includes
   "news, ideas, time & money saving hints to help you work
   at home more successfully"; quite helpful for the serious
   fulltime freelancer
The Indexer: Journal of the American Society of Indexers,
   235 Park Avenue South, 8th Floor, New York, N.Y., 10003
   (semi-annual; annual membership fee includes subscription). Articles on special types of indexes; indexer-pub-
   lisher relationships
Publishers Weekly: R. R. Bowker Co., Subscription Fulfill-
   ment Department, P.O. Box 2017, Ann Arbor, Mich.

48106. The trade journal of publishing; a few freelance ads, but mainly valuable as the source of news in the publishing world

SUPPLIES

In addition to the basic supplies—red pencils with erasers, pens, typewriter, typing paper, paper clips, rubber bands, tape, envelopes or wrapping paper for mailing packages—freelancers may find the following equipment helpful:

Calculator: For efficient accounting, figuring taxes, checking calculations in manuscripts, estimating copy length, and a host of other tasks, an inexpensive pocket calculator is a worthwhile investment for the freelance businessperson.

Copying machine: Copiers for under $100 are easy to use and compact, but the special copy paper is quite expensive.

Numbering machine: These are useful in numbering numerous manuscript pages or index cards; the machine automatically changes number, and can be set to repeat digits up to four times (for carbons). It is easy to set and to use . . . and helps exercise upper arm muscles.

Electric pencil sharpener: This time-saving device can significantly increase an editor's speed when the job calls for heavy copyediting, editing, or rewriting. And as every freelancer knows, time is money.

Telephone amplifier: This device permits you to work with both hands while talking on the telephone. The receiver rests in a cradle and a small speaker and microphone amplify incoming sounds and pick up your voice from a distance. No special installation by the phone company is required.

Telephone answerer: Instead of a regular answering service (listed in the yellow pages under "Telephone Answering Service"), there are answering machines that you attach to your home phone. These are quite expensive—

$100 to almost $900—the phone company must be notified that they are attached (to ensure that your equipment is "compatible" with theirs). They are particularly valuable if you are not home much of the time when you would be getting calls from publishers, or if you are working so hard you do not want to be bothered with answering the phone (or you want to first find out who is calling).

If you cannot obtain any of these supplies, particularly the more esoteric, in a nearby stationery store, write for a free catalog of office supplies and equipment to: Goldsmith Brothers, P.O. Box 227, New York, N.Y. 10038.

Appendix III

COURSES FOR FREELANCERS

Neither author of this book has taken any of the courses in editorial skills at the schools listed below, so we cannot recommend or disparage any of them. Course descriptions can be obtained by sending for catalogs.

School of Library Service, Columbia University, New York, N.Y. 10027 (indexing)

Publication Specialist Program, George Washington University, Library 621, 2130 H Street N.W., Washington, D.C. 20052 (editing, graphics, indexing, writing)

Evening School, Graphic Arts Association, 1900 Cherry Street, Philadelphia, Pa. 19103 (proofreading)

Harvard Summer School, Radcliffe Publishing Course, 10 Garden Street, Cambridge, Mass. 02138 (publishing)

Hunter College, School of General Studies, 695 Park Avenue, New York, N.Y. 10021 (editing)

Center for Publishing, New York University, School of Continuing Education, 100 Washington Square East, New York, N.Y. 10003 (publishing)

Printing Industries of Metropolitan New York, 461 Eighth Avenue, New York, N.Y. 10001 (indexing, proofreading, copyediting)

Department of Independent Study, University of North Dakota, Grand Forks, N. D. 58201 (editing)

Division of Continuing Education, Correspondence Instruction, the University of Tennessee, Communications and University Extension Building, Knoxville, Tenn. 37916 (copyediting)

Division of Continuing Education, Correspondence Study, University of Utah, Box 200, Salt Lake City, Utah 84110 (editing)

University Extension, University of Wisconsin, 432 North Lake Street, Madison, Wis. 53706 (editing)

Appendix IV

SAMPLE COPYEDITING AND PROOFREADING TESTS

These sample tests, created by freelancer Pamela Lloyd, bear a strong resemblance to the tests publishers send out to freelancers. They also resemble actual manuscripts and proofs, although the real thing would never contain so many errors. These tests are designed to help *all* freelancers, old hands and novices alike, to learn their strong and weak points.

There are two sets of tests: copyediting and proofreading. Each set contains four tests, two in fiction and two in nonfiction. "Answers" to the tests are by no means absolute. Every copy editor and proofreader has a different slant on her work, and every publishing house has a slightly different attitude toward style.

COPYEDITING TESTS
FICTION: 1

July 25, 1870

Ive has some narrow ecsapes in my life, but this tops them all.
I had been a normal day with bathing at Steve and Sydneys' next door.
They have hot water! I had came back and started to fix dinner for
my self. I decided to take down the garbage. I saw a Porto Rican
going up the stairs when I was going down. I did'nt think about it.
I had left the door open, as usually do when I empty the garage.
When I returned to the pad I found, this same cat in the bath room,
holding a rather large knife.

He told me to be quiet, that he just wanted to hideout for awhile.
He said the man was after him. I told him to sit down and offered him
a drink.

He drank some orange juice. I was cool, I was trying my damndest
to keep it together. I felt the adrenaline pumping away into my
every vain. He said that the police were after him, cause he had
just beaten somebody up. He said, and I am using his terminology--
some "nigger" had burnt him and that some oldi lady had called the
cops when she hard the fight.

We agreed that the man was a drag, I didn't tell him that I
didn't share his rascist attitude towards black people. He asked me
if I had any money. I said No, and told him about the hard times we
were having. He said that he was a dope friend showed me his tracks
and said that he'll do anything for money while waving the gun in my
face.

I asked him how long he's been on junk. He said, on and off for
7 years, not including the time that he's spent in jail. I asked
him how much he spends a day on junk. He said $36 dollars a day.

He asked about room-mates. I told him about Andrea and Leica and showed him pictures of them, then I told him that they are on welfare and showed him the welfare food that they gave you. He asked me about boy-freinds and I told him about Jose. (He was Puerta Rican too)

He told me that he was into stealing things, and began walking around pad, sort of apraising my paltry and few posessions. He made reference to sevral items of mine, e.g., my giutar, and my radio, and my ring. He found a ten-dollar bill in one of the bureau. I told him that it was Andra's, to pay the kids doctor bill. He pocketted it. He found my pot stash and offered to roll him a joint. He didn't want any. He asked if I had any smack. I didn't. He said that he was sick and started to bending over at the waste, kind of cluching at his stomach. I asked him if he had ever tired the drug rehabilitaion programs. He said that they didn't work.

He asked me if I ever heard of Sharen Tate. Sure, who hasn't? Wierd thoughts ran though my mind. Knivings, rape, torture. I tired to keep it together. He asked me if I was virgin. I said, of course not, what does that have to do with anything?" I figured that a junkie in as bad a shape as this guy probably wouldn't be able to get it up anyway. But he was getting freaky, and I didn't like that at all. He had been in the apartment to long. He heard something outside, and asked me to go out and look out the window to see if it was the pigs.

"O.K. I'll go look if you let me hold the knife. "He handed me the knife. I went to the window, and I turned around he said, "You think, I'm stupid", and clicked out another knive. I gave him back the one that I was holding. There was no sense in fighting him with the knive. I would be torn to shreds in seconds. He kept

FICTION: 1

Designer's note dateline

July 25, 1970 #9

Ive had some narrow escapes in my life, but this tops them all. It had been a normal day with bathing at Steve and Sydneys next door. They have hot water! I had came back and started to fix dinner for my self. I decided to take down the garbage. I saw a Porto Rican going up the stairs when I was going down. I didn't think about it. I had left the door open as I usually do when I empty the garage. When I returned to the pad, I found this same cat in the bath room holding a rather large knife.

He told me to be quiet, that he just wanted to hideout for awhile. He said the man was after him. I told him to sit down and offered him a drink.

He drank some orange juice. I was cool. I was trying my damndest to keep it together. I felt the adrenaline pumping away into my every vein. He said that the police were after him because he had just beaten somebody up. He said and I am using his terminology some "nigger" had burned him and that some old lady had called the cops when she heard the fight.

We agreed that the man was a drag, but I didn't tell him that I didn't share his racist attitude toward black people. He asked me if I had any money. I said No and told him about the hard times we were having. He said that he was a dope friend, showed me his tracks, and said that he'd do anything for money while waving the knife in my face.

I asked him how long he'd been on junk. He said on and off for seven years, not including the time that he'd spent in jail. I asked him how much he spent a day on junk. He said thirty-six dollars a day

He asked about room mates. I told him about Andrea and Leica and showed him pictures of them then I told him that they are on welfare and showed him the welfare food that they gave you. He asked me about boy freinds and I told him about José, who was Puerto Rican too.

au: changes ok?

He told me that he was into stealing things and began walking around the pad sort of apraising my paltry and few posessions. He made reference to sevral items of mine over my gitar, and my radio, and my ring. He found a ten dollar bill in one of the bureau so I told him that it was Andra's to pay the kids doctor bill. He pocketed it. He found my pot stash and offered to roll him a joint. He didn't want any. He asked if I had any smack. I didn't. He said that he was sick and started to bending over at the waste, kind of cluching at his stomach. I asked him if he had ever tired the drug rehabilitaion programs. He said that they didn't work.

au: Andrea ok, as above?

He asked me if I had ever heard of Sharon Tate. Sure, who hadn't? Weird thoughts ran though my mind. Knixings, rape, torture. I tined to keep it together. He asked me if I was a virgin. I said, of course not, what does that have to do with anything?" I figured that a junkie in as bad shape as this guy probably wouldn't be able to get it up anyway. But he was getting freaky, and I didn't like that at all. He had been in the apartment to long. He heard something outside and asked me to go out and look out the window to see if it was the pigs.

"O.K. I'll go look if you let me hold the knife." He handed me the knife. I went to the window, and as I turned around he said, "You think I'm stupid, and clicked out another knife. I gave him back the one that I was holding. There was no sense in fighting him with the knife. I would be torn to shreds in seconds. He kept

au: change comma to question mark?

FICTION: 2

Through the harsh glare of on-coming head lights and the hard,
vynil seatcovers were a far cry from the lambant glow of candle
light and the silky-softness of a warm bed, it wasn't hard for Don to
imagine himself still at Kathys apartment, even as he made the fam-
ilar left turn into the express way. The highway, elevated and isolated above the honeycomb quadrants of the city, filled him with
that strangely-detached and yet secure feeling he often had while
driving late at night leaving his mind free to its phantasies. He
made the few necessary motions to guide the car along automaticly,
while he restructured the scene at Cathy's fine detail, reviewing the
events of the night one by one, in order to draw the last bite of
pleasure from them.

He arrived at the apartment tired and aggravated, because they
still hadn't been able to satisfy that old, bastard Grossman, and
that ment he'd have to design an entirely-new format by the end of the
week. He came in sulking and brooding but from the beginning Kathy
seemed to sense that was wrong. She was beautiful; she kissed hem,
handed him a drink, and led him over to the sofa. She didn't even
ask him about work (thank God!), but she didn't try to distract him
with smalltalk either; she let the firm pressure of her leg besides
his and the savoury odours that were wafting in from the kitchen
take care of that. Simple medicine, and it worked.

Then came the dinner. spanish stew with fried rice, 2 wines,
white and red. . . . delicous. He could still taste the cordialls
that they'd been drinking as they sat around after the meal sharing
joking intimacies. He wanted to make love to her right there on
the couch, but she slipped out of his arms and ran into the bed room,

closing the door coquetishly behind her.

By now, Doug's revery was so complete that when he imagined the warmness of her breasts on his chest as they laid together, he began to feel unmistakeable stirrings in his crotch. "A hard-on, he laughed aloud to himself; but still he could not tear his mind away from its idylic wanderings. It was as though the reconstrucsion of the evening had an inner dynamic, a pleasure principal that required each event to be repeated in sequence. And there remained yet a final pleasure, all be it bitter-sweet one, for his memory to recreate. The image of Kathy sleeping quietly, as he stood in the dark room dressing. What a bitch it was to have to leave.

"What a bitch", he repeated to himself as he glanced at the glowing dial in the dash board; 2:02 a.m. But he'd stayed too long as it was. He had to have the new format by eight a.m. and that ment he'd be lucky to get even the four hours of sleep, that he considered the bare minimum. Fortified spiritualy as he was though, by his memories of the evenings pleasure, and by the more tangable influence of several scotches. Even the prospect of only a nomnal nights rest followed by 8 harrowing hours of trying to placate the imperius Grosman did not cause more than a few superficial ripples in Don's placidity. His gaze shifted slowly from the black mirror of of the River to the jagged sky line of the City. He watched the line as he rode along, drawn by the peaks and abisses of the business district plunge and climb like a graph til it decended finaly to the low stable outline of the squat tenament biulding crowded together in the dark. His thoughts were getting to big for words now, he was thinking in images, pictures evoking more pictures in an endless-rushing stream.

FICTION: 2

Through the harsh glare of oncoming head lights and the hard,
vinyl seatcovers were a far cry from the lambent glow of candle
light and the silky softness of a warm bed, it wasn't hard for Don to
imagine himself still at Kathys apartment even as he made the familiar left turn into the express way. The highway, elevated and isolated above the honeycomb quadrants of the city, filled him with
that strangely detached and yet secure feeling he often had while
driving late at night leaving his mind free to its phantasies. He
made the few necessary motions to guide the car along automaticly
while he reconstructed the scene at Kathy's fine detail, reviewing the
events of the night one by one in order to draw the last bite of
pleasure from them.

He arrived at the apartment tired and irritated because they
still hadn't been able to satisfy that old bastard Grossman, and
that ment he'd have to design an entirely new format by the end of the
week. He came in sulking and brooding but from the beginning Kathy
seemed to sense that was wrong. She was beautiful she kissed him,
handed him a drink, and led him over to the sofa. She didn't even
ask him about work (thank God!), but she didn't try to distract him
with small talk either; she let the firm pressure of her leg beside
his and the savoury odours that were wafting in from the kitchen
take care of that. Simple medicine, and it worked.

Then came the dinner: spanish stew with fried rice, two wines,
white and red . . . delicous. He could still taste the cordials
that they'd had as they sat around after the meal sharing
joking intimacies. He wanted to make love to her right there on
the couch, but she slipped out of his arms and ran into the bed room,

closing the door coquetishly behind her.

By now, Doug's revery was so complete that when he imagined the warmness of her breasts on his chest as they laid together, he began to feel unmistakeable stirrings in his crotch. A hard-on, he laughed aloud to himself, but still he could not tear his mind away from its idylic wanderings. It was as though the reconstruction of the evening had an inner dynamic, a pleasure principal that required each event to be repeated in sequence. And there remained yet a final pleasure, all be it bitter-sweet one, for his memory to recreate. The image of Kathy sleeping quietly, as he stood in the dark room dressing. What a bitch it was to have to leave.

"What a bitch," he repeated to himself as he glanced at the glowing dial in the dash board. 2:07 a.m. But he'd stayed too long as it was. He had to have the new format by eight a.m. and that ment he'd be lucky to get even the four hours of sleep that he considered the bare minimum. Fortified spiritualy as he was, though, by his memories of the evenings pleasure and by the more tangable influence of several scotches, Even the prospect of only a nomnal nights rest followed by harrowing hours of trying to placate the imperius Grosman did not cause more than a few superficial ripples in Don's placidity. His gaze shifted slowly from the black mirror of of the River to the jagged sky line of the city. He watched the line as he rode along, drawn by the peaks and abysses of the business district plunge and climb like a graph til it decended finaly to the low stable outline of the squat tenament building crowded together in the dark. His thoughts were getting to big for words now, he was thinking in images, pictures evoking more pictures in an endless rushing stream.

[Marginal notes: "Au: changes ok?" / "Au: changes ok?" / "Au: 'by end of week' on previous page. Which correct?"]

allegrova

NONFICTION: 1

Mao's Contribution to Marxist-Leninist Ideology

INTRODUCTION

Any attempt to devaluate the extent of Mao Tse-tung's contribution to the development of Marxism-Lenism must at the out-set
come to terms with the nettlesome problem of interperting Maos
writings, determining not simply the content but the intent of Mao's
often-ambiguious and ocasionally conterdictory statements.

The root of the difficulty lays in the fact that " the degree
of allegance Mao has displayed to the doctrines of Marx and Lennon
have varied at different times. . . .He either has insisted on a
rigourous fidelity to the original context of a paticular tenent or
has deliberately distorted or ignored the context his primary
guideline having been his need of the moment."[1] This tenency to
altar theory in accord with the exigiencies of a particular situation is certainly unique to Mao, but in combination with his
decided emphases on practice rather than theory makes the task of
evaluating the real signifigance of his statements unsually difficult.

Unlike Marx and Lennin, Mao Tse-Tung has made no attempt to
systematise his teachings. In 1942
" Marxism-Leninsim, he reminded the partys' intellectuals in 1942, has no beauty, no mystical value; it is
simply very useful....Those who regard Marxism-Leninism
as a religious dogma: Your dogma is less useful than
excrement.'"[2]

1. Arthur Cohen, The Communism of Mao Tse-tung. Chicago & London:
   The University of Chicago Press, 1964).

2. Bianco, Lucien, Origins of the Chinese Revolution 1914-1945,
   (London,University of Oxford Press), p. 79

A man who avows such beleifs will understandably be little concerned
with the over all cohesiveness of his 'theory'.

To obfuscate matters, further there is no distingtion between
Mao, the theoretician, and Mao, the political strategist, in his
writings. Quite often his pronouncments have been shrewdly calculated to achieve an affect completely outside the realm of political
philosophy. For example in order to molify the Soviet Union during
the last few years of his struggle agianst Chang Kai-Shek, Mao was
careful to preserve appearences, and not to challenge the recieved
doctrine. Thus he represented his movement as proletarian even when
it was not..."[2]

In view of these hermenutical problems, it seems that an attempt
to deprive a cosistent political theory from Mao's writings alone
would be to use a Chinese adage "Climbing a tree to look for fish."
Therefore, I will not attempt a detailed analysis of Maos works but
rather have tried to interpert Mao's thought in the context of actual
events in the course of the Revolution, and the early period of re-
socialization that followed it.

The first task in evaluating Mao's contribution of Marist-
Leninist theory is to debunk the popular misconceptions: that Mao's
pheasant rebellion was an original and unique element in the history
of socialist thought.

The demise of the Capitalist Order, and its replacement by the
classless society, was envisioned by Marx as an inevitable result of
economic contradictions inherent in the nature of Capitalism. There

[3]R.N. Carew-Hunt, The Theory and Practice of Communism. (Pengiun
      Books: 1950) p. 261

NONFICTION: 1

 Mao's Contribution to Marxist-Leninist Ideology

INTRODUCTION

Any attempt to evaluate the extent of Mao Tse-tung's contribution to the development of Marxism-Lenism must at the outset come to terms with the nettlesome problem of interpreting Maos writings determining not simply the content but the intent of Mao's often ambiguous and ocasionally contradictory statement.

The root of the difficulty lays in the fact that " the degree of allegance Mao has displayed to the doctrines of Marx and Lennon haxe varied at different times . . . . He either has insisted on a rigourous fidelity to the original context of a paticular tenent or has deliberately distorted or ignored the context his primary guideline having been his need of the moment."[1] This tenency to altar theory in accord with the exigencies of a particular situation is certainly not unique to Mao but in combination with his decided emphasis on practice rather than theory makes the task of evaluating the real significance of his statements unsually difficult.

Unlike Marx and Lennin, Mao Tse-Tung has made no attempt to systematize his teachings. In 1942 "Marxism-Leninism, he reminded the partys intellectuals in 1942 has no beauty, no mystical value; it is simply very useful. . . . those who regard Marxism-Leninism as a religious dogma: Your dogma is less useful than excrement."[2]

1. Arthur Cohen, The Communism of Mao Tse-tung Chicago and London: The University of Chicago Press, 1964)

2. Bianco, Lucien Origins of the Chinese Revolution 1914-1945 (London: University of Oxford Press 1971 p. 79

A man who avows such beliefs will understandably be little concerned with the over all cohesiveness of his "theory."

To obfuscate matters, further, there is no distinction between Mao, the theoretician, and Mao, the political strategist, in his writings. Quite often his pronouncements have been shrewdly calculated to achieve an effect completely outside the realm of political philosophy. For example, in order to mollify the Soviet Union during the last few years of his struggle against Chang Kai-shek, Mao was careful to preserve appearances, and not to challenge the received doctrine. Thus he represented his movement as proletarian even when it was not.

In view of these hermeneutical problems, it seems that an attempt to derive a consistent political theory from Mao's writings alone would be to use a Chinese adage, "climbing a tree to look for fish." More illuminating than Therefore, I will not attempt a detailed analysis of Mao's works but is the interpretation of rather have tried to interpret Mao's thought in the context of actual events in the course of the revolution and the early period of re-socialization that followed it.

The first task in evaluating Mao's contribution to Marist-Leninist theory is to debunk the popular misconceptions that Mao's peasant rebellion was an original and unique element in the history of socialist thought.

The demise of the capitalist order and its replacement by the classless society were envisioned by Marx as inevitable results of economic contradictions inherent in the nature of capitalism. There

3. R.N. Carew-Hunt, The Theory and Practice of Communism (Baltimore, Maryland: Pengiun Books, 1950), p. 261.

NONFICTION: 2

A Kingdom in the Air or the Myth of the Artist as Hero

The myth of the artist-as-hero, a visionary who at once embodys
the spirit of his own time while pointing the way towards a New Age;
a demi-urge who partakes simultaneously both of divine and human
charateristics, and a genius who stands in an imediate relation to
the truth and so is a law unto himself, is such an integral part of
our contemporary attitude toward art that we seldom question it. It
is the stuff of which "super-stars" are made.

The idea that an artist--and specially a musical artist,
is a gifted person, specially endowed from above with abilties beyond
the reach of normal human beings, we accept as fact, as surely as we
accept the fact that the sun moves around the earth, and not vise
versa. Yet just as there was once a time when all men believed that
the earth remained in place while the sun moved in orbit around it,
so there was a time when musicians were considered to be nothing more
than " skilled craftsman who supplied a commodity",[1] a step above
cobblers and masons perhaps, but only a small one.

We owe our present conception of the muscian as artist, and of
the artist-as-hero to the Romantic Era, and particularly to the
musicians of that period, for it was they who proclaimed loudest the
Romantic Message, and made (through the example of their own lives,
the myth of the artist/hero seem real. Within the period between
1889 to 1914, 3 men stand out as a kind of trinity of the Romantic

[1]Schonberg, H.A., Lives of the Great Composers, (W.W. Norton & Co.,
        New York, N.Y. 1970) p.91

[2]I am taking the romantic period, as defined by Longyear, in its
        broadest sense.

faith; three musicains who made unique contributions to the idea of
the artist as hero with out whom the notion would not exist as a vital
part of the contempoary imagination. They are Ludwig von Beethoven,
Franz List, and Richard Wagner. In the lives and acheivements of
these three men we can see the gradual development of the idea of
the musician as an artist, into the idea of the artist-as-hero, and
finally the elevation of the notion of the artist-as-hero to a
mythical level and its incorporation as part of our musical heritage.

We begin with Beethoven the iconaclast. " The difference between
Beethoven and all other musicians before him, beside things like
genius and unparaleled force, was that Beethoven looked upon himself
as an artist, and he stood up for his rights as an artist." The
evidence of this attitude; his arrogance, his contempt for "mobility"
and his ego-mania, has been aduced time and time again by historains
and biographers, it is scarcely possible to say anything at all
about the mans' personal behaviour that is not a cliche. But the
source of Beethoven's belief that he was an artist (and therefore
priveleged in a way that other people are not) has not been given
as much attention as it merits, since it is this inner conviction,
and not the effect of his bad manners was the true foundation of the
myth of the artist/hero.

For Beethoven, "Music was a higher revelation than any wisdom
or philosophy"[4]. In an age that was becoming more superstitous then
religious, Beethoven was one of the first to propose that art,
particulaly music could be Divine. "Beetoven gave the strongest

3. Ibid.

4. David Ewen The World of Great Composers (Prentice Hall, Englewood
        Cliffs, 1962), p.142-143

NONFICTION: 2

(A) A Kingdom in the Air, or the Myth of the Artist as Hero

The myth of the artist as hero, a visionary who at once embodies the spirit of his own time while pointing the way towards a New Age, a demiurge who partakes simultaneously both of divine and human characteristics, and a genius who stands in an immediate relationship to the truth and so is a law unto himself, is such an integral part of our contemporary attitude toward art that we seldom question it. It is the stuff of which "superstars" are made.

The idea that an artist—and specially a musical artist—is a gifted person, specially endowed from above with abilities beyond the reach of normal human beings, we accept as fact, as surely as we accept the fact that the sun moves around the earth, and not vise versa. Yet just as there was once a time when all men beleived that the earth remained in place while the sun moved in orbit around it, so there was a time when musicians were considered to be nothing more than "skilled craftsman who supplied a commodity", a step above cobblers and masons perhaps, but only a small one.

We owe our present conception of the musician as artist, and of the artist as hero to the Romantic Era, and particularly to the musicians of that period, for it was they who proclaimed most loudly the Romantic Message, and made, through the example of their own lives, the myth of the artist/hero seem real. Within the period from 1789 to 1914 three men stand out as a kind of trinity of the Romantic

Schonberg, H.A. Lifes of the Great Composers (W.W. Norton & Co.,
(New York: W. W. Norton & Co., 1970), p. 91

I am taking the romantic period, as defined by Longyear, in its broadest sense.

faith, three musicains who made unique contributions to the idea of the artist as hero, without whom the notion would not exist as a vital part of the contempoary imagination. They are Ludwig van Beethoven, Franz List, and Richard Wagner. In the lives and achievements of these three men we can see the gradual development of the idea of the musician as an artist into the idea of the artist as hero and finally the elevation of the notion of the artist as hero to a mythical level and its incorporation as part of our musical heritage.

We begin with Beethoven, the iconclast. " The difference between Beethoven and all other musicians before him, beside things like genius and unparaleled force, was that Beethoven looked upon himself as an artist, and he stood up for his rights as an artist." The evidence of this attitude; his arrogance, his contempt for "nobility" and his egomania, has been aduced time and time again by historians and biographers; it is scarcely possible to say anything at all about the mans personal behaviour that is not a cliche. But the source of Beethoven's belief that he was an artist, and therefore privileged in a way that other people were not, has not been given as much attention as it merits, since it is this inner conviction, and not the effect of his bad manners that was the true foundation of the myth of the artist/hero.

For Beethoven, "Music was a higher revelation than any wisdom or philosophy" In an age that was becoming more superstitous than religious, Beethoven was one of the first to propose that art, particulaly music, could be Divine. "Beetoven gave the strongest

3. Ibid. Schonberg, Great Composers, p. 916
4. David Ewen, The World of Great Composers, Englewood Cliffs, New Jersey, Prentice-Hall, Englewood Cliffs, 1962), pp. 142-143.

PROOFREADING TESTS
FICTION: 1   CATASTROPHE RAG

You know I can still remember my frist job in a restarant—or maybe it was my second, I don't know but I could hardly play at all: strictly the key of C.

Anyway, it was only my second night and the knots and my stomach were just beginning to unravel. Nobody had thrown any ash trays my way yet; I'd even gotten a tip or two. But then, on my break the owner—a lean, flinty eyed young man, who seemed very serious about everything, but especially money—called me over. He said that he liked what I was doing but "couldn't I shoot the music out a little more?" He went on like that for a few minutes, but I wasn't listening to anything except the veins pounding out a funreal march in my inner ear I got the idea tough.

"Shot the music out a little more,"—and there I was nearly paralysed trying to keep all the bad nots *sotto* voce. I stood their alone at the bar for the rest fo my break, feeling the sweat dampen my stiff, new shirt, cluching my glass of icewater, hopping that maybe, if I squeezed hard enough, my fingers would get frozen to the sides.

"And then I remembered a peice I'd been working on at home. It was rag time—very fast and flashy, with big handfuls of arpegios—I intended to play it just yet; it was'nt ready, think it was called Catastrophe Rag." I hadn't there were a few rough spots that still needed work, and I wasn't even sure if I'd remember it from beginning tò end. But it seemed like my only chance.

So at the end of the break, I marched bravely

back to the piano, blew my hands to warn them up and wham–I struck the opening chords. As soon as I started, I knew something strange was hapening without taking my eyes off the key board I could feel everyone's head turning in my direction, and just as surelv as if I could see them, I knew a few people were smiling, pleased at the cock-eyed rythms coming out of the piano.

It felt like electricity was running through my veins that night—the notes seem to pop up and glow on the keyboard; like they were magnetized, drawing myfingers to the right places at just the right times. I may have played better since, but I can't ever remember playing quite as perfectly. I was more like listening than playing.

I was so excited after that rag I wanted to play for ever—and I nearly did. By closing time the only people still around to listen are the bartender and the bus boys. I fiinally quite when they were turning off the lights, and the hostess, a slim blond not much older than me, said the owner wanted to see me in the back. I don't know what those old cooks must have thought was wrong with me as I strod through the streaming kitchen, grinning like a tipsey politicain.

The owner was sitting in his office, a tiny room, all cluttered up with old menus and advertisments, hunched over a pile of account books. When I knocked he looks up quizziclly at first—like he had just forgotten something.

Then I saw the light in his eyes turn a cool blue. "You're fired." He said it simply and finally, almost like "good night."

"Thanks," I said softly. I took the cheek he handed me and left.

FICTION: 1   CATASTROPHE RAG

You know, I can still remember my first job in
a restarant—or maybe it was my second, I don't
know, but I could hardly play at all, strictly the
key of C.

Anyway, it was only my second night, and the
knots and my stomach were just beginning to
unravel. Nobody had thrown any ash trays my
way yet; I'd even gotten a tip or two. But then,
on my break, the owner—a lean, flinty, eyed
young man, who seemed very serious about everything, but especially money—called me
over. He said that he liked what I was doing but
"couldn't I shoot the music out a little more?"
He went on like that for a few minutes, but I
wasn't listening to anything except the veins
pounding out a funreal march in my inner ear,
I got the idea tough.

"Shot the music out a little more,"—and
there I was nearly paralysed trying to keep all
the bad nots *sotto* voce. I stood their alone at
the bar for the rest fo my break, feeling the
sweat dampen my stiff, new shirt, cluching my
glass of icewater, hopping that maybe, if I
squeezed hard enough, my fingers would get
frozen to the sides.

And then I remembered a peice I'd been
working on at home. It was rag time—very fast
and flashy, with big handfuls of arpegios—I
intended to play it just yet; it wasn't ready, I
think it was called "Catastrophe Rag." I hadn't
there were a few rough spots that still needed
work, and I wasn't even sure if I'd remember it
from beginning to end. But it seemed like my
only chance.

So at the end of the break, I marched bravely

back to the piano, blew my hands to warm them up and wham I struck the opening chords. As soon as I started, I knew something strange was happening, without taking my eyes off the keyboard, I could feel everyone's head turning in my direction, and just as surely as if I could see them, I knew a few people were smiling, pleased at the cock eyed rythms coming out of the piano.

It felt like electricity was running through my veins that night the notes seem to pop up and glow on the keyboard like they were magnetized, drawing my fingers to the right places at just the right times. I may have played better since, but I can't ever remember playing quite as perfectly. I was more like listening than playing.

I was so excited after that rag I wanted to play for ever—and I nearly did. By closing time the only people still around to listen are the bartender and the bus boys. I finally quite when they were turning off the lights, and the hostess, a slim blond not much older than me, said the owner wanted to see me in the back. I don't know what those old cooks must have thought was wrong with me as I strode through the streaming kitchen grinning like a tipsy politician.

The owner was sitting in his office, a tiny room all cluttered up with old menus and advertisments, hunched over a pile of account books. When I knocked he looked up quizziclly at first like he had just forgotten something.

Then I saw the light in his eyes turn a cool blue. "You're fired." He said it simply and finally, almost like "good night."

"Thanks," I said softly. I took the check he handed me and left.

FICTION: 2   LOST AND FOUND

In the dim light Don could make-out long shreds of wall paper hanging of the walls; and a bed, with no sheets or covers. He tunred his shadowy hostess, The sultry pout on her face was gone and she stood on the far corner off the room crigning like a aminal about to be stricken. Feelings of surprise and pity begin to well up inside Dom, than an explosoin in the back of his neck plunged him in to blackness.

Don awake as the first grey rays of the sun were creeping into the room. He reached for the back fo his neck, messaging it gently, wondering if he was badly hurt. It didn't seem like it; there was no blood, and through his whole body felt stiff and sore, nothing seemed to be broken. Still holding his neck, he stood up and glanced dolfully around the dingey room. The bed was the only piece of furniture, in the light it was obviuos that no one had lived there for months.

The chain of event that had placed him there came back all to quickly. Not really expecting to find anything, he checked his pockets. Dan was surprised when he found he still had about a dollar in change an his car keys. The ten dollars though was gone. He shrugged and stumbled towards the door.

The raw morning air revived him a little and as he climbed the stairs some of the more prosiac details of his life began to intrud on his still recovering conscioussness. Like how the *Hell* he was going to get car started and get himself home. As he walked along, threading his way uncertianly back to the car the pain in his neck began to subside. His mood improved. After all, he might have been killed, as it was he'd only lost ten dollars.

It was suprisingly easy for Don to find his way back to the car. What had been a horrifying maze in the confusion of the night, revealed itself to be a few simple turns in the distance of a few blocks. But where was the car. There was the twisted sign where he'd left it, this was the place. But the car was gone.

Maybe the Police towed it away. Don didn't really believe it, but not knowing what else to do he decided to call the station and check. He walked across the street to a dinner that was already buzzing with bleary-eyed drones fortifying themselves with greasey eggs and murdurously strong coffee for the long day ahead. He went to the phone, dialed "0", and mumbled "police to the operator. Don waited while his call was shunted though the labyrinth phone network of the city. "Police, sergeant Alley", the receiver barked suddenly like an intercom. Don gave the sergent his name and a quick explation of what had happened. While the sergeant went to check on the car, Don occupied himself by watching a tatooed young man making unsuccessful attempts to look up the waitress's dress as she bent down to clean up a mess on the floor.

Finally, the sergeant returned to the phone, explaining that, "no there was nothing there about the car, so it was probably stolen, and would Don like to come down now and make a formal complaint".

"Okay," Don acquiesced, "where's the nearest precinct house?"

"Well, from where you are you can walk", the sergeant answered, "just go straight down the the street to your first light, take a left, then go two blocks and . . .

FICTION: 2　　　　LOST AND FOUND

In the dim light Don could make out long shreds of wall paper hanging of the walls and a bed with no sheets or covers. He turned his shadowy hostess. The sultry pout on her face was gone and she stood on the far corner off the room cringing like a animal about to be stricken. Feelings of surprise and pity began to well up inside Don, than an explosion in the back of his neck plunged him in to blackness.

Don awake as the first grey rays of the sun were creeping into the room. He reached for the back fo his neck, messaging it gently, wondering if he was badly hurt. It didn't seem like it; there was no blood, and through his whole body felt stiff and sore, nothing seemed to be broken. Still holding his neck, he stood up and glanced dolfully around the dingey room. The bed was the only piece of furniture in the light it was obvius that no one had lived there for months.

The chain of event that had placed him there came back all to quickly. Not really expecting to find anything, he checked his pockets. Dan was surprised when he found he still had about a dollar in change an his car keys. The ten dollars, though was gone. He shrugged and stumbled towards the door.

The raw morning air revived him a little and as he climbed the stairs some of the more prosiac details of his life began to intrud on his still recovering consciousness. Like how the Hell he was going to get car started and get himself home. As he walked along, threading his way uncertianly back to the car the pain in his neck began to subside. His mood improved. After all, he might have been killed as it was he'd only lost ten dollars.

It was suprisingly easy for Don to find his way back to the car. What had been a horrifying maze in the confusion of the night revealed itself to be a few simple turns in the distance of a few blocks. But where was the car There was the twisted sign where he'd left it, this was the place. But the car was gone.

Maybe the Police towed it away. Don didn't really believe it, but not knowing what else to do he decided to call the station and check. He walked across the street to a dinner that was all ready buzzing with bleary eyed drones fortify-ing themselves with greasy eggs and murderu-rously strong coffee for the long day ahead. He went to the phone, dialed "0" and mumbled "police" to the operator. Don waited while his call was shunted though the labyrinthe phone network of the city. "Police, sergeant Alley the receiver barked suddenly like an intercom. Don gave the sergent his name and a quick explation of what had happened. While the ser-geant went to check on the car, Don ocupied himself by watching a tatooed young man mak-ing unsuccessful attempts to look up the wait-ress's dress as she bent down to clean up a mess on the floor.

Finally, the sergeant returned to the phone, explaining that, no there was nothing there about the car, so it was probably stolen, and would Don like to come down now and make a formal complaint

"Okay," Don aquiesced, "where's the nearest precinct house?

"Well, from where you are you can walk the sergeant answered, "just go straight down the the street to your first light, take a left, then go two blocks and . . .

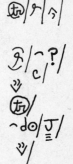

NONFICTION: 1   MARX, ALIENATION, AND IDEOLOGY

1) Put simply, Marx's claim that all German Philosophy is ideology means that German philosophy takes for its basic premisis concepts (substance, essence, consciousness) which are basically religious, ie., matters of faith, and than proceeds to work either downwards to the material life of mankind, or upward to a realm of pure cognition in which the actual life of mankind is sub-sumed. In either case, Marx' objection is the same: instead of starting with a concrete realty (man, history, the modes of production) German philosophy begins with an abstraction and ends finally, in reducing man to a abstration.

The basis of Marx's claim is that" life determines consciousness, conciousness does not determine life." In opposition to the metaphorical concepts that German philosophy uses to understand life (and in particular in opposition to the Hegelian Dialectic) Marx proposes a Material Dialetic, that begins with men " in their real, impirically perceptable process of development under certain conditions. (414 *Early Writings*)

However the polemical tone of Marx's work on *Alienated labor* seems to suggest that there is a value judgement, or at least a philosophical appeal to principle other then that of the modes of production in his use of the term "alienation," but at first the discussion seems to be a purely economic one: a description of the process by which the worker's object becomes seperated from him. It is not until Marx begins to explain the way in which the alienation of the workers object from himself, becomes ultimately the alienation of his own labor from himself that we get a strong implication of the ought; not simply that the worker is separated from his labour, but that it *ought not to be so.*

Marx seek to justify this by a discussion of men's "specieslife," and it is here that our supicions that Marx is appealing to a principal beyond the "material life of man is confirmed. He explains "species-life" thusly:

In the mode of life activty the entire character of a species lies; and free conscious activity is the species character of man . . . In the treatment of the objective world, therefore, man proves hiself to genuinely a species-being. This production is his active species–life. Through it nature appears as his work and his actuality. The object of labor is thus the objectification of mans species-life; he produces himself not only intellectually as in consciousness, but also actively in a real sense and sees himself in a world he mad. In taking from man the object of his production, alienated labor takes from him his species-life, his actual and objective existence as a species." (*EV* 294)

Marx's claim is here made explicit: alienated labor does merely separate man from his products, it robs him of his existance. Though Marx claims that this aspect of alienated labor is "derived from two previous ones," (the separation of "nature from man, and man from himself." (EW 294), there is a conceptual leap hidden in this notion of "species-life," one which, despite Marx' spesious reasoning, must place him back in the relm of idealism.

In the arguments that Marxes descriptoin of species life, he asserts that one the one hand "Conscous life activity distinguishes man immediatly from the live activity of the animal. Only thereby is he a species-being. but then also that "he is only a conscious being since he is a specious being. These is parently circular.

NONFICTION: 1 MARX, ALIENATION AND IDEOLOGY

(1) Put simply, Marx's claim that all German Philosophy is ideology means that German philosophy takes for its basic premises concepts (substance, essence, consciousness) which are basically religious, ie., matters of faith, and then proceeds to work either downwards to the material life of mankind, or upward to a realm of pure cognition in which the actual life of mankind is subsumed. In either case, Marx' objection is the same: instead of starting with a concrete realty (man, history, the modes of production) German philosophy begins with an abstraction and ends finally in reducing man to a abstraction.

The basis of Marx's claim is that "life determines consciousness, conciousness does not determine life." In opposition to the metaphorical concepts that German philosophy uses to understand life (and in particular in opposition to the Hegelian Dialectic) Marx proposes a Material Dialectic that begins with men in their real, empirically perceptable process of development under certain conditions (414 *Early Writings*).

However, the polemical tone of Marx's work on *Alienated labor* seems to suggest that there is a value judgement, or at least a philosophical appeal to principle other then that of the modes of production, in his use of the term "alienation," but at first the discussion seems to be a purely economic one: a description of the process by which the worker's object becomes seperated from him. It is not until Marx begins to explain the way in which the alienation of the workers object from himself becomes ultimately the alienation of his own labor from himself that we get a strong implication of the ought; not simply that the worker is separated from his labour, but that it *ought not to be so.*

Marx seek to justify this by a discussion of men's "specieslife," and it is here that our supicions that Marx is appealing to a principal beyond the "material life of man is confirmed. He explains "species-life" thusly:

In the mode of life activity the entire character of a species lies; and free conscious activity is the species character of man. . . . In the treatment of the objective world, therefore, man proves hiself to genuinely a species-being. This production is his active species life. Through it nature appears as his work and his actuality. The object of labor is thus the objectification of man's species-life; he produces himself not only intellectually as in consciousness, but also actively in a real sense and sees himself in a world he mad. In taking from man the object of his production, alienated labor takes from him his species-life, his actual and objective existence as a species (EW 294).

Marx's claim is here made explicit: alienated labor does merely separate man from his products, it robs him of his existence. Though Marx claims that this aspect of alienated labor is "derived from two previous ones," (the separation of "nature from man, and man from himself" (EW 294), there is a conceptual leap hidden in this notion of "species-life," one which, despite Marx' specious reasoning, must place him back in the relm of idealism.

In the arguments that Marx's description of species life, he asserts that on the one hand "Conscous life activity distinguishes man immediatly from the live activity of the animal. Only thereby is he a species-being, but then also that "he is only a conscious being since he is a specious being. These is patently circular.

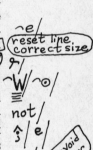

NONFICTION: 2

Neitzsche and Eternal Recurrance

The doctrine of the eternal return: "that all things reccur eternally, and we ourselves too; and that we have already exited an eternal number of times, and all things with us," (p. 332) is according to Nietzsche, the only way we can escape from the "dungeon" of the past. For even if the will to power is powerless in the face of the past; if our antecedants are determined wholly apart from ourselves, then the will to power is not supreme, and all our willing is contingent on what we have been bequeathed, and so is merely 'revenge.' In Nietzsche's words; "This indeed, is what revenge is: the will's ill will against time and its 'it was'." (252) For Nietsche, the only way the will can redeem itself is to redeem us from the past. "To redeem those who lived in the past and to recreate all 'it was' into 'thus I willed it'--that alone should I call redemption." (p. 251)

This is precisely what Nietzsche hopes to accomplish with the teaching of the eternal return. If all is will to power, then the past too must come under the will's control. When we will *something* we will it eternally: This is the teaching of the eternal recurrence, and it is through this uniting of the will and destiny that Nietzche seeks to overcome the contingency of existence.

The circularty of this process immediately apparent: since what we will at this moment has already been willed at some previous moment, in what sense can we say we have "willed it thus." Apparently, only in the sense that what is both cause and effect, as every moment of willing must be) is beyond the law of contingency.

Nietzsche extorts us both to forget and remember the teaching of the eternal return. Perhaps what he means is that we should remember what we are the sole creaters of value, since our will is destiny; but that we should forget that since our will is destiny, our creation is our enslavement. What Nietzsche seems to be advocating *practically,* is that we lose ourselves in the euphoria of willing.

This seems to be the meaning of *The Other Dancing Song,* in "Part III" of *Zarathustra.* Here the lady Wisdom, until now a rival for Nietzsche's affections, is no where in sight. She has been overcome by the Lady Life, to whom, Nietzsche now whispers the "sweet nothings" of the eternal return, and proclaims "Then life was dearer to me than all my wisdom ever was" (p. 339).

To return to the philosophical problems generated by the teaching of the eternal recurence; though it is perhaps unfair to criticise Nietzsche on solely philosophical grounds, *philsophically* speaking, the idea of the eternal return intead of refuting nihilism and determinancy, merely restates them.

Nietzsche asks us to loose ourselves in the creation of value, while at the same time the doctrine of eternal return—through its assertion that all value is determined eternally, undermines teh very possibility of their being any value.

On the other hand, regarding the relativity of value—that there is no truth, only perspectives: though Nietzsche can be credited with recognizing the paradox generated by a self reference of this principle,(i.e. if we claim that there are only perspectives, then our claim itself is merely a prespective.) he cannot claim to have solved it, by forgeting it.

NONFICTION: 2

Nietzsche and Eternal Recurrance

The doctrine of the eternal return "that all things recur eternally, and we ourselves too; and that we have already exited an eternal number of times, and all things with us" (p. 332) is according to Nietzsche, the only way we can escape from the "dungeon" of the past. For even if the will to power is powerless in the face of the past, if our antecedents are determined wholly apart from ourselves, then the will to power is not supreme, and all our willing is contingent on what we have been bequeathed and so is merely revenge. In Nietzsche's words "This, indeed, is what revenge is: the will's ill will against time and its 'it was'" (252) For Nietsche, the only way the will can redeem itself is to redeem us from the past. "To redeem those who lived in the past and to recreate all 'it was' into 'thus I willed it' that alone should I call redemption" (p. 251)

This is precisely what Nietzsche hopes to accomplish with the teaching of the eternal return. If all is will to power, then the past too must come under the will's control. When we will something we will it eternally. This is the teaching of the eternal recurrence, and it is through this uniting of the will and destiny that Nietzsche seeks to overcome the contingency of existence.

The circularty of this process immediately apparent: since what we will at this moment has already been willed at some previous moment, in what sense can we say we have "willed it thus." Apparently only in the sense that what is both cause and effect, as every moment of willing must be is beyond the law of contingency.

Nietzsche exhorts us both to forget and remember the teaching of the eternal return.
Perhaps what he means is that we should remember what we are the sole creators of value,
since our will is destiny but that we should forget that since our will is destiny our creation is
our enslavement. What Nietzsche seems to be
advocating *practically* is that we lose ourselves
in the euphoria of willing.

This seems to be the meaning of *The Other
Dancing Song,* in Part III of *Zarathustra.*
Here the lady Wisdom, until now a rival for
Nietzsche's affections, is nowhere in sight. She
has been overcome by the Lady Life, to whom
Nietzsche now whispers the "sweet nothings"
of the eternal return and proclaims "Then life
was dearer to me than all my wisdom ever was"
(p. 339).

To return to the philosophical problems generated by the teaching of the eternal recurrence,
though it is perhaps unfair to criticise Nietzsche
on solely philosophical grounds, *philosophically*
speaking, the idea of the eternal return, instead
of refuting nihilism and determinancy, merely
restates them.

Nietzsche asks us to loose ourselves in the
creation of value, while at the same time the
doctrine of eternal return—through its assertion that all value is determined eternally undermines the very possibility of their being any
value.

On the other hand, regarding the relativity of
value—that there is no truth, only perspectives:
though Nietzsche can be credited with recognizing the paradox generated by a self reference of this principle, i.e. if we claim that there
are only perspectives, then our claim itself is
merely a perspective, he cannot claim to have
solved it by forgeting it.

INDEX

Boldface numbers refer to Chapter 7 entries; see page 128 for explanation.

font, type, 124, 214
 wrong, 113, 125
footnotes, 47, 67–69, 82–83, 104–
 105, 108, 171–172
 to tables, 69–70
foreign languages, 79
 countries' names, 37–38
 dictionaries, 87, 217
 editorial work, 182–183
 persons' names, 140–143
Fowler, H. W., 217
freelancers, vii, 1–2, 5–8, 35–37, 90–
 95, 131–132, 174–175, 184–185
 advantages, 5
 complaints, 6–8, 27–30, 188
 experienced, 8, 27, 85
 full-time, 2, 5
 lists of, 22
 novice, 8, 9–32, 40–41, 95–96,
 132–133, 169, 171–172, 179
 organizations, 7, 11, 132–133, **203,
 210**
 out-of-town, 30–32, **203**
 part-time, 2, 5, 9–10, **193–194,
 198–199**
Freelancer's Newsletter, 12, 26, 28,
 190, 220
"Freelance System Works for Us," 7
front matter, 214
*Funk & Wagnalls Standard College
 Dictionary,* 56, 59, 216
furniture, home office, 25
 deduction for, **189, 191–193, 199**

galleries, art, 179
galleys, book, 4, 97–107, 171, 214
 cast-off, 133
 copyediting, 105
 corrections, 106–110
 revised, 111
 see also margins, galley
Gay, Robert M., 218
gazetteers, 87, 127
"Going Rate," *Freelancer's Newsletter,* 12, 26
government, U.S., 12, 179, 219
 see also Internal Revenue Service
Gowers, Ernest, 217
Graff, Henry, 220
Graphic Arts Association, 223
grammar, 33–35, 42, 45, 95, 103

errors, 13, 107
 texts, 35, 87, 127, 217–218
Great Britain:
 freelancers, 7, **204**
 spelling, 56, 59, 63–64, 98, 170
 surnames, 140–143
Gross, Gerald, 219
Grosset & Dunlap, 219

hairline marks, 102, 107
Hammond Inc., 219
Hammond's Historical Atlas, 219
Harcourt Brace Jovanovich, 220
Harper & Row, 217
Harper's English Grammar (Op-
 dycke), 217
headings, column, 69
headings, table, 69
heads, running, 110, 215
heads, text, 80, 98, 108, 214
heating bills, deduction for, **197**
Hebrew names, 140–143
Henry, Leon, Jr., 219
Hill & Wang, 217
Holt, Rinehart, 219
Home Book of Quotations (Stevenson), 219
Home Office Guide (Henry), 219
Home Office Report, 220
homonyms, 151
hospitalization, 209–210
houses, home office in, **195–196**
houses, publishing, 214
Hunter College, 223
Huntington Library, 176
hyphens, 53, 55, 63, 74, 76–77, 82–
 83, 100–101, 113, 156
 repeated, 121–123

ideas, indexing, 135, 146–149, 153
illustrations, 108, 151, 177–182
income, business, 25, **188–189, 205**
 adjusted gross, **205, 208**
 gross, 5–6, **206, 208**
 records, **188–189, 210**
income averaging, 209
indents, hanging, 71, 214
indents, paragraph, 67–68, 71, 74,
 113
Indexer, 132–133, 220–221